A LIFETIME AFFAIR

LESSONS LEARNED LIVING MY PASSION

Stephanie Ann Lynn

Birddog Productions

Fall Creek, Wisconsin

A LIFETIME AFFAIR
Lessons Learned Living My Passion
Stephanie Ann Lynn

Birddog Productions
PO Box 306
Fall Creek WI 54742-0306

Edited by Susan Carter

Cover Design by Deb Usher

Copyright © 2011 by Stephanie Ann Lynn
Printed in the USA
Library of Congress Catalog Card Number 2011914599
ISBN 978-0-9838550-0-2

First Printing 2011

Cover Photo: Stephanie atop Little Billy holding her first trophy

Dedicated to every little girl or boy, no matter their age, whose dreams of riding horses have given them something to look forward to. To the parents and loved ones who dropped them off at the barn, took them to lessons, drove long miles to horse shows and allowed such dreams — thank you — keep dreaming.

In memory of my father, Melvin E. Lynn Jr., an unwitting and sometimes unwilling accomplice in it all.

Table of Contents

Foreword

I am so proud of Stephanie, more than I can say in words. Not only does she share her passion in a book about her love for horses, she shares her lifetime experiences to influence children and parents and to show readers how horses can nurture people helping them to live successful lives. Her own self-determination illustrates how anyone can succeed in life, with or without horses!

I will never forget the day that I met Stephanie. I went to her parents' farm in Eau Claire, Wisconsin, to look at a horse to buy for a client. I was so impressed with her riding; I had to have her work with me! I thank God this happened in my life.

Stephanie was the first person I groomed to be exceptionally successful in the horse industry. In my past 41 years as a professional horse trainer, competitor and instructor, many young people come to me and say "I want to be a horse trainer." So few make it. Stephanie did. Now she has impressed me with a new talent to write! You will keep turning the pages of this book, wanting to know what next happened in her "lifetime affair" with horses! I am so proud of her. Horses have brought her a successful career, quality of life, happiness, and for you or your children, a mentor for new equestrians.

In 2009, I proudly cheered from the stands as I watched Stephanie win at the AQHA World Championship show in Sr. Pleasure Driving. Stephanie is a wonderful lady and deserves all she dreams of in life. I hope that she will influence you, as she did me. There is nothing greater than to have horses a part of your life. Use Stephanie's stories to Follow Your Dreams.

Lynn Palm Pittion Rossillon

Acknowledgements

Many people have helped me along my way. First I must thank my parents, Sally Resh Lynn for her never-ending support and gentle shoves in the right direction and Melvin E. Lynn for teaching me that anything was possible if I worked hard enough. Thank you to my sisters, Cindy, Deb and Jennifer, along with their families, for their support, tolerance and critical eye. And, of course my husband, John Beck, for putting up with me as I endeavor on another hair-brained scheme. His devotion to me and my wild antics keep me grounded as I flitter off, suit-case in tow, to another horse show, the precise destination too much for him to keep up with.

This book could not have been possible without the help of many people who have impacted me in ways beyond belief. I have been fortunate to have many mentors influence my life. This collection of stories includes just a small representation of the various individuals who helped shaped my career and to whom I owe a great deal of gratitude. My special thanks to Jerald Murphy, fondly known to all as Murph, Jan Phillips Hasart, Jerry Erickson, Dianne Eppers, Sandra Vaughn and a very special thanks to Lynn Palm. Without her assistance and coaching, many lessons would have been left unlearned, or worse, learned incorrectly. Thank you for being tough and always demanding excellence.

The book itself is the result of the hard collaborative work of many individuals. Thanks to Susan Carter, my editor and advisor, you can read this book with some semblance of order. Susan's help and guidance has been tremendous as I set out to learn more lessons and make more mistakes. Any errors in grammar are mine and mine alone, hard fought to use against her best advice. Carol Carlson, thank you for "flushing out" my ideas and offering your well thought out first impressions. Thank you to my sister, Deb Usher, for the incredible design and cover work. Finally, you get credit for your talent.

It is impossible to thank everyone who has touched my heart, urged me to go forward and encouraged my advancement. For all that I have not mentioned, know that your guidance is appreciated and I am forever grateful for your influence.

Little Billy and Stephanie in 1969

The horse that started
the whole affair.

Introduction

Lucky Girl

According to my mother, I went from riding in my stroller to riding horses. On a whim, my mother enrolled our entire family in horseback riding lessons after attending a gala at the saddle club across the road from the local stable. Begrudgingly, even my father, a man who startled from the touch of a dog's nose, learned to ride. I was too young to sit in a saddle on anything other than Prince Harry, our toy horse perched in the kitchen corner. Children were not allowed unattended in the barn yard, so until I turned five, I watched from the comfortable seat of a four wheeled stroller. When I finally sat on a real horse, my life was altered and my path determined. Horses would become my life's pursuit.

I don't remember dreaming of horses or playing with horse dolls as a kid but I do remember riding. We were lucky to have a local stable that boarded horses, providing their feed and care. The stable also gave lessons and offered barn rats like me a place to hang out. At the time, my parents had no idea the effect that such an innocent gift would have on my life.

At the stable, there were kids of all ages. From first graders to college aged girls, we all rode together. The older girls were very impressive; independent, they radiated freedom and were the essence of the liberated teen. As the youngest of the group, I always looked up to them, mesmerized. What I could not know then, was that someday little girls would look up to me with the same gaze in their eyes.

My life as a coach started very young. It began in an atmosphere that was warm with the sweet smell of horse sweat, the clomping of hooves hitting hard ground and the soothing sound of horses' giant teeth munching on hay. Everyone helped each other. It was just what you did; you held the horse, helped put the halter on, pushed the saddle over the top or tightened the girth; you helped clean the stall, adjusted the stirrups, consoled and celebrated.

Friends were always there to catch the horse when he bucked me off, and to remind me of the fall I took when a horse show win made my head too big. We laughed and we cried and we grew up. It was a fairytale childhood for a little girl who loved horses. As a kid, I was never happier than when I was at the barn. I was truly a lucky girl!

While struggling to learn how to handle these big magnificent creatures I came to love horse shows. I started competing in simple classes riding behind my big sisters, stirrups so long I could not reach them, pigtails bobbing, happy to show my missing teeth through a big smile. As my riding skills matured, so did my goals and by the age of seventeen I could no longer afford to compete at the level I aspired to. Turning professional seemed the natural thing to do.

I traveled from coast to coast competing at local horse shows and national competitions including World Championship Shows. At home in Texas, I created my own little hang out for kids who loved horses and, before I knew it, I was hauling kids from my Texas ranch to horse shows across the country. I taught kids who had never sat on a horse and kids who were World Champions and kids who were older than I.

The lessons learned have provided a wonderful life; one filled with thousands of fond memories and lifelong friendships. Relationships based on the common scent of horses have taught me to dust myself off when I am down and shared in the glory of the happiest days of my life. How blessed I am.

The following are a few tales from the lessons learned on my journey. The people in the stories are some of the best people in the world. As my dad used to say – they are good people. I cherish them, the memories they have helped create and the life they have afforded me.

I am truly a "lucky girl"!

**Little Billy and Stephanie (in Cowboy hat turned)
getting lunch 1970**

Waiting with a friend;
the friend well
worth the wait

Chapter 1

A Child Waits

At the tender age of five, I finally got to ride a real horse. The springs on Prince Harry, the black and white stallion on a stand, were stretched from use. Thankfully, I had reached the accepted age for riding lessons. Still the youngest of the family, I was a tag along, a nuisance to my big sisters. They were eight and nine, big girls, and like every younger sibling – I wanted to do everything they did – as they did it.

When it came to riding, my two older sisters, Cindy and Debbie, had been in lessons for a couple of years. Riding with kids their own age, they were walking, trotting, and even cantering on horseback, trading secrets from horse to horse.

My oldest sister, Cindy, often rode Sweetheart; the barn favorite with smooth gaits, flaxen mane and a pretty face. Tiny was a tall bright red sorrel whose effortless gaits also made him a barn favorite. Debbie, often stuck on Lady, complained about the fat little red roan mare's cantankerous attitude. She may have been slow, but if you cued her correctly, she loped off with ease, floating across the ground.

Everyone longed to ride Dream: a beautiful and gentle Palomino mare. Her soft yellow color mirrored her personality. Bing was a big gray gelding who liked to lay down in the sand to cool off taking his rider down with him! Buck, as his name implies, was a Buckskin gelding, raw-boned with a giant head and heart to match.

I was introduced to Cricket at my first lesson. Tall, almost black, he had a kind dark eye and a long neck with a soft fluffy mane that was easy to hold onto. Cricket stood quietly for me as I learned to groom, pick hooves, saddle, bridle and eventually mount. His long legs swung slowly over the ground in an easy four-beat flat-footed walk.

Cricket moved off dutifully, accepting his job with resignation. He walked around and around the arena ferrying me past the gate without stopping as other horses did. He walked circles, walked over logs and walked wherever I pointed him. But that was the problem! All he did was walk – I thought he was a plug, incapable of going faster. Having carried thousands of kids before me as they learned to ride, I decided he was just too old and tired to go any faster. *Plus*, his legs actually creaked when he walked. I suppose that is why they called him Cricket.

We all rode at Murphy's Stable. Located in Elk Creek, it was a short drive from our home in Eau Claire, Wisconsin, and the only stable of its kind in the area. The owners', Fritz and Murph, were local icons. Fritz, short and rather portly, could often be seen wearing a tent dress. She was a jolly ole gal who ran Murphy's stable like the modern day CEO. She always knew what was going on, recognized the guilty from the innocent and could distinguish lazy kids from go-getters. If you had a question, a request or just had to get it done, Fritz made it happen.

Murph was a small man; an experienced horseman, his formidable personality commanded respect. What he lacked in height, he made up for in stature. Strong, tough and feared by all, he was not a man to be questioned – especially by a five year old kid.

Murph had been training horses and students for 20 years earning a solid reputation as a winning instructor. His students, master horsemen, consistently won top honors when competing at the state and regional horse shows. Both students and horses were exceptionally well schooled. Above all, Murph's students were noted for the awards they took home in the Stock Seat Equitation classes.

Defined as the art or act of riding a horse, equitation refers to the riders' position while on the horse and involves their ability to ride correctly using the proper aids. A good equitation rider is always in balance and maintains a correct position in every gait while possessing a commanding, but relaxed, presence, able to direct the horse with nearly invisible cues. The equitation *class* is designed to test the rider's ability as a horseman.

It was Murph's job to teach us to be good horsemen. Through his tutelage, we learned proper form, terminology and parts of the horse. Murph taught us what tack (equipment) to use and how to care for it. He taught proper and effective aids (signals) used to control the horse while we handled them. Murph taught us how to feed, clean and care for the horses. Yet more than anything, he taught us about the character, the temperament, the very substance of the horse, deepening our understanding of this majestic soul.

A horseman is more than a man riding a horse. A true horseman has a relationship with the horse based on respect for the animal; an ability to communicate with the animal on a subliminal level gaining the acceptance, cooperation and most importantly, the trust of his horse. It is truly a combination of art and feel.

Indeed a true horseman in every aspect of equestrianism, Murph's authority went unquestioned. So when I whined about my lack of progress with Cricket, my complaints fell on deaf ears. Sitting in the back seat of my mom's wood-paneled station wagon on the way home from the barn, Mom said I would do what Murph told me to do or I would not ride. It was just that simple.

And so I did. For a year I stayed at the walk. I practiced posting. Posting is rising out of the saddle and gently sitting back down in rhythm with the horses stride *at the two-beat diagonal trot*. But I was walking! Up and down, up and down, up and down.

Slowly I practiced without the benefit of lift from the bounce of the trot, my little legs getting stronger; finding their proper place in the stirrups, heels down toes up, directly under the shoulder. My hands were figuring out how to control the horse, learning to be soft with the tender mouth I held between my small fingers. Developing a sense of the strength and power beneath me took much practice.

Up and down, up and down, up and down; I practiced and practiced at the walk, posting, walking, and developing a connection with the giant animal under my saddle. Steering became easier; soon Cricket stopped, backed and walked wherever I asked him to go.

Upon arriving at the barn one early spring day, Murph told me to get Tiny out of his stall. Glancing warily, I noticed his craggy face had a slight upturn, a twinkle sparkling in his eye. I scurried quietly to Tiny's stall flush with anticipation, unable to temper my thrill. I had longed for the day when I would finally be able to ride someone — anyone — other than Cricket and do more than walk.

Had the day finally come when I could go faster, maybe even gallop, and feel the breeze on my face? After agonizing, pouting, begging and being discouraged, I hoped this would be the day I finally would get out of the tiresome walk. In my mind, I had suffered through a year of tedious, painful and completely *unnecessary* delay.

But to Murph, it was a natural progression. He never lost sight of his main objective: to teach every one with aptitude to become true horsemen. As horsemen, we had to learn to put the needs of the horses in front of our own. The horse had to know I would not flop on his back if I fell behind the rhythm or pull on his mouth when I lost my balance. By the time Murph finally allowed me to test my abilities at the trot, it was no big deal. Without missing a beat I rose and fell in step with the horse's footfall. In no time I cantered like my big sisters — but not before the horse could trust me.

Murph was more concerned about the harm I could do to his horse than any potential fall and resulting injury to me. He cared more about the welfare of the horse than about collecting a check from my parents. If pressured by a parent, he would rather snub the earnings than mollycoddle a student through a lesson. Most interested in his animals, Murph insisted horses came first.

He taught patience, the importance of detail and above all respect — for the horse. I learned that this horse, this giant animal, relied on me to do the right thing. To Murph, a horsemen's greatest accomplishment was to earn the trust of this majestic soul.

Fundamentals learned in those first years of slow and tedious lessons laid the groundwork and built a foundation on which I endlessly *strive* to become a horseman. It is the basis on which I attempt to gain the trust of every one of the hundreds of horses that I have trained, sat on or come in contact with. The habits Murph instilled are still intact today and have served as a guide throughout my life, with and without horses.

Mastery skips no steps. Up and down.

Up and down. Up and down.

**Little Billy in 1969 with Stephanie in the saddle
sisters Debbie and Cindy standing**

After watching our girls' talents and interests in horses grow or wane, Murph's prophetic words to me as he nodded to a very young Stephanie were:

"That's your rider."

Sally Lynn

Chapter 2

Passion

The fall of 1968 brought my seventh birthday and my first competition. A small open show, it was held across the street from Murphy's Stable at the Bit & Spur Club's show grounds. Fritzie and Murph sponsored the show and offered special classes for their students who did not own a horse. Kids enrolled in Murphy lessons could enter and show on one of Murphy's school horses. Classes corresponding to age and skill levels ensured a class for everyone. Since my sisters and I were students, we were able to show on the school horses. Other riders, some students and some not, competed on horses they owned. Murph entered me in the 8 & Under Walk-Trot class on Tiny, the big red gelding who taught me to trot.

The judge conducted the competition. His directions were conveyed to the announcer who then broadcast the judge's requests over the loudspeaker. Contestants entered the show arena and rode single file around the white fenced arena. After walking and trotting both directions of the ring, we lined up in the center of the arena. The judge then walked the line and individually asked each rider to back their horses as he approached for final inspection. Ribbons were given through sixth place; blue for first, red for second, yellow for third and so on. When the announcer called my name out third, I continued to stand in line, unaware of the procedure. Finally the ring steward directed me from the line up to the gate where a girl extended a bright yellow ribbon high over her head.

The ribbon, the most beautiful (and only) ribbon I had ever won, had a large rosette with a picture of a horse's head in the center. Beautiful bright yellow and white streamers hung long with the date and show's title embossed in gold letters. I gladly accepted the ribbon and beamed with delight.

My father would later say that the yellow ribbon earned for third place effectively stole my heart. But Dad sealed the deal when in the spring of 1969 the Lynn family purchased Little Billy. For $350.00 Little Billy came with a saddle, bridle, halter and a heart of gold. Mom, bit by the bug, had successfully convinced Dad to take the plunge. Horse shopping with Murph, she wanted the beautiful little black mare with a baby doll head and keen alert eyes. Murph scoffed at the mare, "too high strung," he said pointing instead to a big plain headed bay pony. "That's the horse for you" Murph said after scooting under his tubby brown belly a time or two.

Murph convinced Mom her girls needed a packer; a safe and secure horse. The Lynn family needed something sturdy enough to handle the four girls, not some flighty high spirited black beauty who could not handle stress. Already aware of the social stigmas that surround horse people, Mom feared the pony Murph picked out would be dismissed as the ugliest horse in the barn by fellow riders. But Mom would not argue with Murph — his word was final and Little Billy was indoctrinated into our family like a fluffy puppy.

Billy made the family Christmas card for the next two decades eventually teaching not only all four Lynn girls, but countless others, the joy of riding. Best of all, my older sisters and I could now join the group who carpooled to the barn every night after school to ride. Before Billy, I only went to the barn on lesson days, now I went as often as Mom would allow. Fortunately I grew up during a time when grade school homework did not exist. Nor were there organized sports or extracurricular after school activities for girls. I spent one year as a Brownie and discovered quickly it was not for me. I would rather feed horses, clean stalls and sweep barn aisles than cut out paper dolls and sell cookies. I would even voluntarily help Mom with my baby sister if it meant going to the barn.

Kids at school teased me and called me "horse." Among the tallest of my class, I often wore my long hair in a pony tail or braids and classmates knew I rode horses. The stable offered a welcome relief from childhood jibes. At the barn, being tall was a benefit. Long legs, advantageous to riders, also helped me fit in with the older kids. Most importantly, my new best friend Little Billy lived there. I never knew his head was ugly, his neck too thick, or his body too coarse. To me, he was beautiful – the best horse in the whole world. His kind heart comforted me many nights as I sat in his manger and shared the day's events.

Arriving at the barn one afternoon following school, something felt wrong. A dark green pickup truck with side utility doors standing open blocked the big overhead entry. The usual hum was absent when I stepped through the squeaky wooden door on the side of the barn. I heard no laughter coming from the grooming area, no feet clomping on the paved aisle as one of my friends led a horse to or from its stall and no sound of Murph scolding one of his unruly young boarders. The barn was entirely too quiet; a dark gloom hung in the air. I crept around the corner, moving toward the only sound I heard; hushed murmurs coming from the indoor arena. A group of students and boarders huddled around the door to the arena looking at a black horse in the middle of the arena.

Whispering to one of the girls, I looked in with fear. Dr. Flynn, dressed in big pocketed coveralls, held a stethoscope to the belly of Carolyn's horse, Fancy, the beautiful and flighty black mare Mom first wanted. Ann, one of the teenage girls, explained Dr Flynn was listening for gut movement. Unable to hear any guttural movement, Dr Flynn concluded Fancy was colicky. Incapable of passing stool, Fancy appeared to have an impaction in her intestines, blocking a bowel movement. The practice of colic surgery still many years away, Fancy's best hope for survival included a combination of ancient treatments.

The vet pumped a mixture of oil and water into her stomach attempting to push something through the 100 feet of intestines. A sedative would help keep her more comfortable and hopefully prevent her from rolling. The potential for a twisted intestine greatly increased if she laid down and rolled. Walking a colicky horse distracts them from rolling or thrashing around. So we all took turns walking Fancy to give Carolyn a break and allow Murph a chance to take care of the other horses. Keeping her up and walking grew increasingly challenging. As the night wore on, it became more difficult to distinguish between discomfort and fatigue.

I called Mom and begged her to let me stay through the night. Fancy was very sick and I did not want to leave the barn. The pit in my stomach ached and I desperately wanted to stay. It did not seem fair for me to go home to my bed while a horse fought for her life. Of course Mom refused to let me stay. She agreed to pick me up later than usual, but Fancy was *not* my horse and I had school in the morning. That night, gazing at my yellow ribbon hanging against the pink flowered walls of my bedroom, Fancy's eyes stared back, haunting my sleep. Grateful it was not Billy's life that hung in the balance tonight, I still feared for the fate of a fellow friend and stable mate.

Bursting through the barn doors after school the next day, I raced to Fancy's stall. From my height running, the stall appeared empty. Stopping with a jolt, I grabbed the bars on the stall and standing on my toes, peered into the stall. Fancy's head shot up. She had been quietly snoozing, chin resting on her bent front legs, flecks of straw stuck on her flared nostrils. My clamoring down the barn alley must have awoken her. Fancy's ears pricked up and her eyes earnestly met mine.

Thank God! She stood up and shook the straw off her belly, walked to me and gazed hungrily at me for food. Looking around her stall I saw fresh piles of manure — a good indication her intestines were working. Fancy was going to be okay. Relieved, I rubbed her head then bounded down to Billy's stall to share my joy. Leaning against the manger, I snuggled close to his broad forehead: Billy welcomed the affection. I wrapped my arms around his thick, cresty neck and gave him a big hug. He did not care why he got attention and I did not care if he had a big plain head. He was my best friend and I needed his comfort.

This would not be the last night that a horse's eyes would haunt my sleep. Later, I would have to make decisions with life altering consequences for horses in my care. Nights were spent tending to the needs of sick horses in surgical centers or vet clinics at home and on the road. Worse yet, were the nights spent outside the stall of a sick horse, one whose monetary value did not warrant the cost of the life saving surgery. The eyes, always the eyes, tugged at my heart. Whether they made the grade and were surgical candidates or not, their eyes haunted me just as Fancy's had back at Murphy's Stables.

Decisions were never made easily; their ramification's grave. No matter the outcome, the horses beneath the decisions, all tore my heart. There has always been something about a horse that rocks me to my very core, becomes my essence. It is beyond my control. Dad always thought I chose horses, but in reality, horses chose me. It took my father four decades, but in the end, he understood it was not the yellow ribbon that stole my heart.

There is something about the outside of a horse
that is good for the inside of a man.

Winston Churchill

**Little Billy and Stephanie with new friend Laurie Vaughan
holding the reins before a Tandem Bareback class
at a 1971 Bit & Spur Open Show**

The advantage of having older sisters, their cunning behavior had an unintentional benefit, planting the roots of a hearty spirit.

Chapter 3

Grit

Imagine a little girl, head bent down, walking through a field. On her shoulders, she carries a horse's halter. The halter, a heavy leather headpiece, is bigger than she and the attached fat cotton lead rope drags close behind. Stretch pants tucked into boots too big, she chases after a big brown horse who trolls for fresh greens in a pasture full of flora. As the little girl gets close, the horse trots away innocently, as if looking for greener grasses.

That was me — forever trying to catch up. My two older sisters taunted me with independence that I did not yet have. They were a head taller than me, a few years older and enjoyed liberties I only dreamed about.

"Of course," Cindy and Debbie told Mom, "Stephanie can ride with us anytime." What they didn't tell Mom was if I wanted to tag along, I had to get there on my own.

Finally, catching the horse, with an occasional can of oats to help, I wrestled with his unwieldy head. As I tried to put a halter on him, the horse earnestly sought more grass, walking away. Eventually coming up for air, I snagged the opportunity to slip the halter over his nose. With his warm muzzle gently nudging me along, we walked to the grooming area, now vacant after my sisters saddled up and left me. After brushing his back then hoisting the saddle over my head and onto the horses back, I cinched the saddle as tight as I could. Provoking me by rubbing his huge head against me, I struggled to put the bridle on as he continued to use me as a scratching post. Finally ready to ride, the horse stood quietly while I crawled up the fence, shoved my foot in the stirrup and climb aboard.

Ditched again — I struck out across the road to ride.

Maybe I would gallop through the fields pretending to be a hunter (sans gun or ammo) or perhaps into the arena for a make believe horse show. Finding a trail, I pursued my antagonists. As I became faster, my sisters and their friends grew craftier. Because they were a group and I rode solo, they easily surrounded me in games of cowboys and Indians trapping me and calling me out. Laughing, they rode away excluding me from their tribe of merriment.

Wandering back on trails by myself, I met another young girl riding alone. She lived down the road from Murphy's Stable and invited me to her house. Laurie and her pony, Queeny, rode in their small pasture when not on a trail ride. Laurie and I played with our ponies jumping logs on the trail, riding in tandem together on one pony or the other and taking them to the creek where we built a private fort. Soon the familiar games of my elders did not matter. I had a new friend and concocted a scheme of my own.

Laurie, happy to have someone to ride with, kept asking me over to her house. They actually *lived* on their little farm and had a multitude of farm animals. We gathered up geese, chickens, goats and finally horses before we were allowed in the house for supper. At my house in the city, we were permitted only a cat and a dog. This was big fun — albeit work — and good training. The animals were always trying to get away from us and avoid capture. Time at Laurie's house prepared me for horse show classes like egg and spoon, ride-a-buck and goat tail tying. After collecting eggs, jumping bareback on horses to round up geese and manhandling goats by grabbing around their necks and tails to wrestle them into stalls, classes at the horse show were quite civilized.

In egg and spoon, riders were given a spoon to put the egg on – no chickens to move. Holding the egg steady in one hand and reins in the other, riders followed the direction of the announcer. The last rider remaining with an egg won! In ride-a-buck, all the riders had to do was ride bareback with a dollar bill tucked under their leg. Again, the last rider with a dollar won the class. My sisters found goat tail tying disgusting and dirty. Goats were tied to the end of a rope on a stake. The riders ran to the stake on horseback, jumped off, grabbed the goat, who boldly tried to escape capture, and tied a ribbon on their tail. A task much easier than catching goats running free in a tree-lined field!

Laurie, unlike my sisters, welcomed me and my hanging around the barn. In the process of having fun with Laurie, I learned much about life on the farm. Everything we did at Laurie's enriched skills that in time helped me in the show ring. The next year, with several more classes added to my roster, I won the 13 & Under High Point Buckaroo at the Bit and Spur Horse Show. I even made the local paper.

Although my sisters lacked the desire to compete for the hi-point, they appreciated my ability to do so. The competition gave me a goal, validating the value of my efforts and confirmed what I already knew; I was obsessed with horses. While they would rather play games, ditching me at every opportunity, laughing all the way, I developed a work ethic. The wily pranks Cindy and Debbie played with their friends served me well. They may have outfoxed me in the race to leave the barn but when it came to taking home the biggest prize, I won.

Never did anyone have to tell me when to practice, help me with the saddle, bridle or even to catch the horse. Rarely did I need to be told when to be ready to show or to perform the required gait when asked. I did not need someone to fix my hair, pin my hat on or fill out an entry blank. I did not seek attention, nor require approval from my idolized big sisters. Tenacity replaced helplessness and gave birth to an independence previously only viewed from afar. Strangers became allies, uniting determination with purpose. Struggling to keep up, to be taller, to do what the older kids did, cultivated a resolve I would later need in the sometimes ruthless world that would become mine.

It is our ability to deal with challenges

that will determine who we become.

**Stephanie accepting a blue ribbon on
sister Debbie's horse, Dusty, in 1973**

When Deb stopped showing up at the barn, I took over the
reins of Dusty. Having out grown Billy, opportunities for
advancement were not squandered. A fierce determination to
progress rose from the very games that Deb and Cindy played
and I barged through the door left open by Deb's lack of
interest.

**Little Billy and Stephanie practicing jumping
at home on the Little Ponderosa**

We shared a bond I would only come to understand much later in life. Billy helped make clear lessons that were better learned early than late. Even his refusal to buy into some of my schemes, tough to swallow at the time, had deep significance that served as a guide for a tough career choice.

Chapter 4

Experience

"He's all mine!"

The first year I did not have to share "Little Billy" with my sisters was a glorious year. My oldest sister had all but quit riding. Debbie, three years older than I, moved up to a new Quarter Horse. An *almost* beautiful gray mare, Debbie named her new horse Dusty. The youngest of the four girls, Jennifer, did not yet ride.

Billy was a big red bay pony with a bulging white blaze down his face, tall white socks on his legs and a neck as thick as his girth. A cross between an American Quarter Horse and a Morgan, he barely squeaked under the measurement for pony classes. Billy and I rode all over the *Little Ponderosa*, the stable we moved to after Murph's retirement. We rode through the fields, down the hill to the Rodeo Arena, across the creek and wherever the wind took us. Now that I did not have to share, I taught him all sorts of new tricks — one of which was how to jump. He loved it. Billy appeared to be a natural; ears pricked forward, tucking his knees under his chin, he sailed over bales of hay, barrels or any other odd combination of sticks and poles I rode him to.

Seeking recognition for our new found talent, I desperately wanted to show Little Billy over a course of jumps. It seemed only fitting that at our last horse show of the season Billy and I would make our debut in the children's Hunter class.

The year was 1972. I celebrated my 11th birthday in the fall. That year, we ended our show season with the Fall Harvest Show in La Crosse, Wisconsin. Kids, ponies, horses as well as their families packed up their gear, heading south for the weekend. You might have thought it was 500 miles from home, not 50. But at my age, any trip that required a stay overnight was a big deal. At the Fall Harvest Show, we stayed two nights in a *real* hotel – the Holiday Inn.

The show started early Saturday morning with classes divided between two arenas. The jumping events were held in the Grand Prix arena, a large fenced area of cut grass. The western classes showed in a dirt arena with a brown board fence around it. The show ended Sunday night with Championship Jumping events in the Grand Prix arena and Championship western events in the western ring.

Except for Billy and me, everyone in our barn showed only in the Western arena. Keeping my aspirations to myself, I secretly entered Little Billy in the Pony Hunter Class. The class was offered for youth riders less than 12 years of age riding ponies who measured under 14'2 hands or 58".

Show day dawned cool and brisk. My mom and I arrived early and together we fed Billy and Debbie's horse, Dusty. Breakfast eaten and stalls cleaned, I saddled up Little Billy and headed for the practice pen. Through the fog, colorful autumn leaves were abundant all around us. They were not alone shaking in the breeze. The crisp air made many of the horses feel frisky as they cantered around the practice pen. Nostrils flaring, blowing air and snorting from freshness, Billy and I warmed up beautifully. Billy jumped all of the practice jumps, unpainted posts and rails, with ease, just like he did at home.

Pony hunters jumped the lowest fences making the class the first of the day in the Grand Prix arena. After studying the course, I entered the arena when my number was called. Eight beautiful jumps designed to mimic obstacles encountered in nature were set strategically on the lush field of green grass. Some were made of Birch rails; some looked like bountiful flower baskets and some like natural hedges. All were decorated with brightly colored flowers, corn husks and fresh greenery in front of giant wing standards.

The whistle blew and I was off at a hand gallop. I cantered a courtesy circle and headed for the first jump. Now the cool air felt good blowing on our faces. My faithful Mom stood outside the arena — watching with anticipation as Little Billy and I galloped toward the first fence. As we approached I gave him an extra push along with a free rein to jump.

The beauty of the course, however, was a bit of a shock to my partner, Little Billy. As we approached the jump he put on the brakes sliding to a stop. I was stunned. Now what? I turned him away, picked up the canter and started toward the jump again. Again, Billy stopped. A third time I picked up the canter and a third time Billy stopped.

I turned to try again. As the tears started to flow, I heard a whistle blowing. Not understanding what the whistle meant, I started toward the jump again, determined to make Billy go over the fence. Jumping horses are allowed only three major disobediences before being disqualified, and we now had three refusals. Over the loudspeaker, the announcer asked me to leave the arena as I galloped towards the fence. After a fourth refusal, finally hearing the announcer, I walked to the exit gate, crushed and devastated. My poor Mom felt my despair. We just couldn't believe it. Billy and I had worked so hard. Mom knew how much competing in the class meant to me.

Embarrassed and deflated, I now had to go back to the barn and be confronted by all my riding buddies. They would ask how I had done, taking secret delight in my failure while pretending to care what had happened. Crying my way back to the barn, Mom scolded Little Billy. Flabbergasted, Mom kept asking Billy why he wouldn't jump.

"What is wrong with you?" she asked. "Why wouldn't you just jump over the little jumps?"

But I knew what had happened. The jumps were smaller than those we practiced at home. I knew it was not the fence height. Billy was a country boy and the grandiose jumps, pomp and circumstance, were just too much for Little Billy. He had never seen so many variations of beautiful jumps. Giant wing standards held the rails, lavishly decorated, frightening Billy like monsters on the attack. Billy had only jumped posts and rails at home with an occasional bale of green hay thrown in for variety. The fancy flowers, green carpeted roll tops and red and white painted brick walls were just too much and threw Billy for a loop. He was afraid and I had not properly prepared him for the threat he faced in the show ring.

Back at the barn, I changed Billy's tack, took off the English saddle and replaced it with the heavy western saddle. Donning a Cowboy hat, back in my familiar western tack along with my favorite bright yellow vest, Billy and I jogged to the western arena. We ended placing well; reserve champions in our division of the Stock Seat Equitation class. It was familiar and it felt good but it was not what I came to do.

I was only 11 and did not fully make the connection at that moment, but many lessons were learned that day. Although I did not win, I did not lose. I did not take home the trophy, but I still took home the prize:

Experience. It's what you get when you don't get what you wanted.

Stephanie with All About Lark winning the Senior Pleasure Driving at the 2009 AQHA World Championship Show. Pictured with her are trainer, Kevin Dukes, his daughter, Mattie, Mark Stevens, owner Ginger McCaleb, Alice Holmes and Lisa Ligon.

Many failures have led to my success — each experience playing a part in developing traits I depend on without thinking, experiences that have led to opportunities beyond my wildest dreams at eleven years of age.

Kevin Dukes had more driving horses than he could show in 2009. Hired to "catch" drive, I met All About Lark, two nights prior to showing him in the biggest show of his career. Unafraid to fail, the possibilities are endless.

Photo Courtesy of Georgi

**Jayne (Kaiser) Plumer receiving
another blue ribbon from Fritzie
at the Bit & Spur**

"The true test of character is not how much we know how to do, but how we behave when we don't know what to do."

John W Holt Jr.

A healthy dose of fear kept me in check as a child growing up: fear of having the animal I loved taken away from me, fear of somehow hurting the animal I loved, fear of losing the animal I loved and fear of losing the trust I fought so hard to earn.

Chapter 5
Growing Up

Every time riders enter the show ring, they are being judged. Every mistake made is committed in front of an audience. Friends, there to catch you when you fall back at the barn, now find fault with every move you make looking for an opportunity to beat your go (performance). Family, whose hard-earned dollars support you, cheer you on from the sidelines silently hoping for a return on their investment. Coaches, whose livelihood depends on your success, scrutinize each step in an attempt to make your next performance better. From the time I entered my first competition, my most meaningful lessons would be learned in front of an audience.

Showmen are always being judged; by childhood pals who want to win as badly as they, alongside parents who want their children to beat them. Spectators, judging for their own reasons, watch from the sidelines ready with a catty comment. Even at the barn, there is always someone waiting to burst your bubble. And finally, the showman steps into the arena in front of a judge whose job it is to sort through the riders, pick the winners and place the class.

Murphy's Stable's biggest show of the show season was the Minnesota State Fair. Held in St. Paul, the Minnesota State

Fair concluded Labor Day Weekend with grand celebrations. Fireworks, beer tents, bands and the area's largest Stock Horse Show brought the fair to an end. Entrants traveled hundreds of miles to compete for prize money, trophies, and bragging rights from the area's largest all-breed equestrian event.

By 1973, Murph had retired and sold his stable. A young student of his, Jan, had taken over his "stable" of students, hauling, coaching and mentoring this unruly bunch. In keeping with the Murphy tradition, the prize most coveted by the students was awarded Saturday night during the Stock Seat Equitation Championship class.

After competing in their divisional classes, the top five riders in each division were invited back to ride again in a Championship class with multiple judges. It was an honor and a thrill to ride against the other winners on Saturday night. The atmosphere sizzled with energy as the qualifiers prepared to show. Riders who did not qualify enviously cheered for the contenders, some bitterly, but most were excited to be a part of a winning team.

Jayne, one of the older girls at the stable, had won the Championship trophy twice in the past. The State Fair was her show and she always did well. She rode in the 14-17 division and I rode in the 13 & under. This particular year she qualified for the Championship Class by placing second in her class. Another rider in our group, Julie, had won the preliminary class in the older age group and felt certain the Championship trophy was finally going home with her. Having played second fiddle to Jayne for years, she convinced herself this was her year.

The Saturday evening performance began with an eight-horse hitch of Clydesdales pulling the famous Budweiser wagon. Fans roared as they tore around the "Hippodrome," which was the official name of the coliseum. The Midwest's equivalent of Madison Square Garden, this night it always filled to capacity.

Boisterous spectators elevated the noise level. Bright lights shone from high above the ceiling and reflected off high white walls of the Hippodrome. It made for an electric atmosphere.

The buzz in the Hippodrome continued even after the thunderous team ran out of the arena. Horses felt the energy, excitement and tension in the air. Riders, already nervous in anticipation of the class, were on edge as they jogged through the entry gate.

Jayne and her horse, Champ, rode in confidently with poise. The team thrived on attention and loved the opportunity to be in the spot light. Jayne's stark white blazer atop stylish navy chaps with contrasting white buck stitch stood out prominently against the solid wall of the arena. Champ, a 16-hand bay gelding holding his head high, nearly pranced with pomp while Jayne radiated self-assurance. A blind judge could not miss this dynamic duo.

Julie's horse was particularly sensitive to the buzz in the arena and Julie reacted in kind. Leaving her composure at the gate, she nervously held her reins tight, giving her horse cause for concern. Leaning forward with obvious tension, Julie's posture drew negative attention to her problems and distinguished her from the other riders, her anxiety evident by her position.

After the riders performed on the rail, they lined up in the center of the arena for one last challenge. Each entry was asked to canter out of line, stop and back. Jayne and Champ, first to perform, loped out easily and stopped and backed with accuracy. Julie's horse, high strung by nature, startled at her cue and jumped out of line after feeling Julie's leg. With reins too tight, she hauled back on the horse's mouth demanding a stop. The gelding stopped, his mouth gaping and backed showing his resistance to Julie's rough commands. The judge's marked their cards and riders were placed in reverse order from sixth through first.

My sister, Debbie, earned fifth place with her gray mare, Dusty. On a borrowed horse, I was called out for the third place. Second place went to a girl from South Dakota leaving both Jayne and Julie standing in the line-up. A hush fell in the arena as everyone awaited the results to be called. Finally, the winner was announced — Jayne and Champ won the Stock Seat Equitation Championship class for the third year in a row.

Left with no prize at all, Julie stormed back to the barn. She threw the reins down, left her horse in the middle of the alley and stomped around. On a tirade, she tossed her expensive hat on the ground, hit her horse, blaming him for her loss then kicked her bridle out of the way. If she wanted attention she definitely got it.

With ten of us sharing a tack stall, her behavior did not go unnoticed. While she ranted and raved, the rest of us unsaddled our horses, then took care of hers. Dismayed, not wanting to get in trouble ourselves, we picked up after Julie and hurried off to celebrate. And we had reason to celebrate — five of the six top honors came home with our crew.

Julie's reaction to her loss defined her in my eyes. She continued to ride with our group but without the respect she once had. Although she was several years my senior, she never again received deference from me. She lost the courtesy of respect during her angry outburst and the obvious disregard she showed her horse after a loss. Julie broke one of Murph's Cardinal Rules — horses get credit for wins and riders take blame for losses. Julie was beating up the wrong individual.

Miles clicked by quickly on long drives home spent laughing at mistakes made. Dreams were conceived marveling over great rides, while acts of stupidity provided scripts for comic relief. Admiration, rarely given in public, was generously granted in private. Horse show conduct offered fodder for small talk pitched over wheel barrows, manure spreaders and shared chores. Performances, good and bad, were probed in a never ending journey to the winners' circle. Every discriminating detail was dissected in an effort to gain knowledge, lighten your own load or provide some necessary humor.

Wins were remembered by a few, losses by fewer; but conduct was remembered by all. It became evident that to be memorable, you had to be either very good or very bad. There was never a question which way I wanted to go — I always wanted to be good — the best if I could make it happen.

In every competition, the obvious goal is to win — and I wanted to win! But what I wanted most was to be respected. Looking back, it was a strange way to grow up, but grow up I did, in front of peers, trainers, mothers, judges, bystanders, movers and losers. Some championed my successes while others cheered my failures.

Missed leads were placed last, long practiced patterns forgotten upon entering the show arena were disqualified and back numbers forgotten at the stable prevented entry at the gate. Cones knocked over, jumps refused, failed attempts all were made more embarrassing by the ever critical eye of the public watching from the other side of the fence.

No matter who tried to take credit for my wins - it was my behavior that would always be mine and mine alone to be judged accordingly.

Control your behavior;

Control your destiny.

**Jennifer on Frank, Stephanie with her Ryon saddle on Weslee,
Sally standing with Sheba**

Break time in the arena shortly after moving to Texas and
establishing my training business. Shown sitting on one of my
first training horses, Weslee's owner, Charlotte would become
a veteran customer winning many awards, and remains a good
friend to this day.

Chapter 6

Satisfaction

I was thirteen years old when my stable mate Jayne got a brand new saddle. It was a Billy Royal, hand tooled and loaded with the latest in Sterling Silver. Etched and raised in the center to look like berries, the Sterling sparkled next to the dark oiled leather and silver rolled cantle unique to the saddle maker.

To say that I was envious would be an understatement. My saddle was as old as the hills and handed down after my sister, Debbie, chose cheerleading over horseback riding. I had moved onto a new horse, Vandy, a lanky young mare whose tolerance for my teen-aged temperament matched my tolerance for waiting. I wanted a new saddle too, but try as I might, it was just not in the cards. I had three sisters and they had hobbies and Grandma was sick and Jennifer had camp and Cindy was graduating and the house caught on fire and Jayne was eighteen years old, for God's sake. Defeat, never an easy pill for me to swallow, fostered solemn determination.

The 1970s were a great time to be a kid. I could ride my bike anywhere in town without a worry from Mom. Cars, big and slow, were few and far between. Being the third daughter of four, I held the perfect place in my family. Jennifer, the youngest, required more attention than I. Cindy and Debbie, now sixteen and seventeen, were into bigger stuff than their bothersome little sister. Preserving the peace, I stayed quiet, tried not to make waves and avoided trouble or attention at all costs. I followed the rules, rode as often as possible and plotted a course to acquire a new saddle.

Taking every odd job available to a thirteen year old girl in 1975, I shoveled drive ways, swept sidewalks and did household chores for vacationing neighbors. I exercised horses for fellow boarders in their absence, watered plants and cleaned kitty litter boxes. I walked dogs, groomed horses, cleaned stalls, took down cob webs and babysat kids.

I hoarded money, saving until I gathered a few hundred dollars. Far short of what it would take to buy a saddle like my friend Jayne's, yet encouraged by my stash, I started looking at catalogues. Cutting out pictures of potential saddles, I found one perfect for me. The price seemed reasonable so I offered up my savings to help pay for the saddle.

Almost ten months had passed since Jayne received her saddle. September rolled along bringing another birthday for me. What better gift for a soon-to-be fourteen year old girl than a brand new saddle? Unfortunately, my dropped hints went unnoticed. Mom didn't give the pictures even a cursory glance – not a good sign. I resorted to begging but my requests fell on deaf ears.

Fourteen is an insignificant birthday to most teenagers; but, for a horse show kid, it has serious implications. At fourteen, kids move into the toughest age division for youth riders. The youngest of the 14-18 division, some must also suffer the various and utterly apparent developmental changes, or lack thereof, that occur between the ages of 14 and almost 19. A fourteen year old girl can be at a serious disadvantage in the older age group.

My fourteenth birthday was a sad day. A class win would most likely be a long time in coming — and there was no mention of a new saddle, not even an I-owe-you, a present my parents developed after discovering how expensive it was to outfit a horse. Resolute, I continued to take any cash paying job working to increase my stash.

Spring in Wisconsin is a renaissance. Spiny sprigs of bright green grass courageously struggle to sprout through the dirty snow. Tulips vividly bloom brightening gardens around town. My lungs filled with the fragrance of lilacs as I rode my bike home from school one fine spring day. Peddling through puddles of melted snow, the rooster tail from my wheels threw cold water on my back. Yikes that was chilly! Looking at my hand-me-down bike it suddenly dawned on me — there might be another way to get a new saddle.

The Lynn family had a deal: Mom and Dad bought our first bike. For our second bike, each child paid for one third and Mom and Dad picked up the remainder. After that we were on our own. Cindy long ago bought her own bike and Debbie cruised around on her second bike, when she wasn't fighting Cindy for the car. I rode — hmmm — Debbie's *first* bike. Mom and Dad had never purchased *any* bike for me.

Knowing a saddle like Jayne's was out of the question, I found one for far less money. Scouting through magazines I discovered plenty of reputable saddle makers. Choosing one with a price tag I hoped would meet Dad's approval, I approached my parents with a new deal.

Recognizing a saddle would cost much more than any bike, I offered my stash to help pay for the new saddle. My earnings were enough to pay for well over half but I would still need help. If Mom and Dad paid the balance, I promised to never ask for money for a bike. At last, a deal was struck and the saddle ordered.

The saddle I found was made in the heart of horse country. The Ryon family name is steeped in the tradition of Texas saddle makers. Hand tooled in Fort Worth, the saddles were thrown on the backs of the best horses in the country. From cutting horses to pleasure horses, the saddles were known for their functional craftsmanship. The new saddle was far less fancy than Jayne's, and by now, two years newer. But it was not a hand me down. The saddle was all mine and I had earned the right to be proud of its purchase.

In the years to come, I swung that saddle on hundreds of horses. It was a show saddle before becoming a work saddle – the first of many tools of my trade. My Ryon saddle helped earn my first dollars in the horse business providing a means for me to carry out my profession. But more than anything, it served as a source of satisfaction – the reward – a fine compensation for the efforts spent. Using available resources, I fulfilled a wish and unleashed a means to gratification I would not otherwise have known. By denying a desire, my parents, once again, gave me a gift. Providing for myself, I found satisfaction in what first appeared to be a hardship.

Satisfaction comes easily to those willing
to persist in their pursuits,
no matter the result.

Jane Katelynn Usher
A second generation of Lynn girls eagerly awaits her turn to show

All we need to be happy is something to look forward to.

Jeanne (Perlich) White, a student, working her horse in a very busy warm up pen alongside many others just like her

To be singled out in a crowd,
recognized among the scores of other riders,
satisfies a hunger,
often, more than a ribbon.

Chapter 7

Compliments

The day that I turned 16 my mom took me to the DOT to test for a driver's license. Parallel parking my mother's four door tuna boat with ease, I returned home a licensed driver, grabbed the keys to the 1968 VW Bug no one wanted and headed for the barn.

As soon as I could, I borrowed my dad's big old black car, a front wheel drive two-door Toronado, and backed it up to our two horse bumper pull trailer. Taking care of myself had become a way of life and my best defense against arguments from adults, especially my parents. I learned to hitch and unhitch the trailer, test running lights and, trailer in tow, back out of any spot I pulled into. It didn't take long before I was loading Easy Brick into the trailer and driving myself to horse shows. Staying within the region, I went to as many horse shows as my parents would allow.

Easy Brick, my handsome chestnut gelding, came to the Lynn family after a roller coaster ride with Vandy. Purchased as a two year old for a know-it-all thirteen year old, Vandy had learned to push me around. Herd bound, we had one wreck after another as Vandy continually took me back to the gate refusing to leave the other horses. Mom finally agreed to let me find help and we contacted Jerry Erickson, a young trainer living sixty miles from us. Jerry, a recent graduate of the University of Wisconsin at River Fall's Animal Husbandry Program, also trained Jayne's horse. Jayne, now enrolled in the same curriculum, allowed me to stay with her and hauled me back and forth from Eau Claire to River Falls. I spent a summer at Jayne's apartment, going to the barn, riding, helping with chores and going to horse shows. It was an emotional year fraught with disappointment and frustration until Jerry convinced my dad I needed a new horse.

After an extensive search, Jerry found Easy Brick in Iowa. Dad had not given Jerry a very big budget, but Jerry found another great horse for the Lynn family and Easy Brick soon had a new home. Easy and I spent the first months we owned him riding with Jerry in River Falls. At fifteen, I lived with and like the college students who treated me as their servant. The exposure taught me about the responsibility that comes with independence. Even before becoming a licensed driver, I helped with any chore, from hitching the trailer to pulling it around the barn for loading to assuming driving duties when a driver became overwhelmed with fatigue; I tried to pull my load.

When spring broke, Easy Brick came home to Eau Claire. Although not the fanciest horse at the shows, we were a good team and won our fair share. Confidently preparing him by myself, I loved the freedom that came with the newly acquired driver's license. Independence earned while living away from home was not lost and I anxiously set out to prove our mettle. I immediately struck out for new destinations — horse shows previously unattended. It was at one such show that I received a gift that forever changed my outlook.

Most of the regular horse shows schedule a lunch break. It is a break during the competition that allows judges time to eat and exhibitors' time to practice riding in the show arena. Lunch breaks give the horses an opportunity to see the scenery and get familiar with their surroundings. It also gives riders an opportunity to scope out the competition.

Riding Easy Brick during a lunch break in Jefferson, Wisconsin, a well known trainer rode up alongside me, brought her horse to a walk and introduced herself. Although she needed no introduction on my part, she asked my name and inquired about Easy Brick and me. As we walked side by side around the arena, she continued to ask questions. Unsure why she wanted to talk to me, a little nobody, I awkwardly answered. After all, she was a famous trainer with a host of students. Her actions surprised me.

After a few question filled laps, Dianne complimented my riding. A young trainer from Illinois, Dianne won the All-Around Youth in the nation in 1970 and since then had made several AQHA World Champions. She and her husband had an established stable of students and horses and were well known in the winners' circle. The prestigious trainer told me I did a nice job preparing my horse and looked good in the saddle. Twenty questions and twenty minutes later, Dianne invited me to ride in her *group*. Her expression of approval, curious in origin, left me exhilarated. Highly skilled competitors, her students took home most of the blue ribbons.

We parted ways to continue our schooling, but I departed changed — and charged. Elated, something was different for me. The pride I felt was immeasurable. I understood the importance of the time taken as well as the potential jeopardy Dianne placed on her reputation by acknowledging me. Unafraid, Dianne seemed not to notice my inferior rank in this ring of elite riders. Instead, she took time away from her distinguished paying clients to pass along a compliment to ME, a nobody. With Dianne's flattery as an ally; I rode off on a high.

The flattery came with some disappointment at the knowledge that we could not afford her services. I knew Dianne had been recruiting — looking to add to her stable of winners. But that in itself, her belief that I could be a winner, was enough to put me on cloud nine. The acknowledgement and praise coming from this highly respected trainer motivated me for years to follow. When discouraged while riding some skag trying to turn it into a star, I would remember her words. Her praise inspired me to strive to be the best rider I could be.

Dianne continued to watch me grow and became one of my most valued mentors. Her advice is always sound, given freely, compassionately and honestly. A few years ago I told her this story. She had no idea how significant her words, spoken thirty years ago, were to me still today. Not as virtuous as she, her benevolence continues to inspire me to find the good and recognize it in everyone. It costs so little to give a compliment — the encouragement it provides can truly change one's life.

Dianne Eppers giving advice to her granddaughter, Nyah Kearns, at a horse show in Florida. Naturally empathetic, Dianne leans down to meet Nya's eyes.

Compliments are gifts,

give them generously and often.

The joy they deliver is a reward beyond measure.

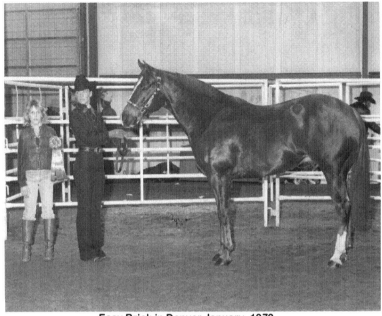

Easy Brick in Denver January, 1979
Accepting a blue ribbon at the horse show prior to the sale.

Hopes and dreams are dashed so quickly. Our lives can change drastically in a matter of seconds; some things are out of our control, others completely within our control. Yet the outcome is still the same: our lives are changed.

Chapter 8

Words

It was a typical January morning in Wisconsin. The sky, pitch black and dotted with stars, was still hours from sunrise. A big moon shone and reflected off the snow lighting the barnyard like day. Temperatures hovered just below zero all night, dropping further as daylight approached. The wind, howling out of the west, kept slamming the trailer door shut on my backside as I tried to load one more bale of hay. Easy Brick was bundled up under heavy winter blankets and stuffed into the little two-horse trailer, happily munching on breakfast in the midst of a manger filled with hay.

Denver was our destination: it was my mother's and my first cross country trip with the horse trailer. My dreams of showing around the country died with the dawning of both an economic downturn and the realization that Easy Brick was not enough horse to get the job done. Time spent in preparation to graduate high school early now wasted, I moved on to Plan B. Lacking the wherewithal to fund my dreams, Easy Brick had been consigned to auction. The decision had not been an easy one, but in the end, I decided to sell my only asset of value. We consigned him to the largest horse auction in the west. The first sale of the New Year, it was held in conjunction with a prominent horse show in Denver, Colorado.

Established in 1906, the National Western Stock Show gathered the best livestock in the west and provided a market for their sale rivaling those held in Chicago and Kansas City. The Quarter Horse show and sale were added in 1944. Attendance continued to grow, making the annual event a hot spot for livestock sales and the first premier Quarter Horse show event of the season.

Ten minutes out of the driveway, unable to get coffee to her lips without it splashing onto her lap, my mom questioned our sanity. A storm was brewing in the west and the National Weather Service was threatening to close Interstate 80. We had 1000 miles to travel and I was anxious to press on and make our destination. The radio played low, suppressing the news to my mom, as she tried unsuccessfully to nap.

We were driving a single cab one-ton dually pickup truck with a two horse bumper pull trailer. The truck, manufactured to carry a substantial load in its bed, carried the light trailer attached to its bumper like a bucking bronco carrying a monkey on its back. The stiff suspension and dual rear wheels, intended to absorb the load, instead made for a bumpy ride offering no traction in wicked winter weather. The wind screaming across the highway added to the instability of our rig making it unsafe for the road conditions.

Four miles per gallon meant we stopped for gas often. At every stop, Mom talked to truck drivers coming from the west. The weather was truly treacherous. Although the roads had not yet been closed, truckers all warned us to take heed. The further west we traveled the more stern their warnings became. Mom desperately wanted to stop. Truly afraid, she had never driven a truck and trailer. I had enjoyed my license for just over a year. Having spent her life in Wisconsin, she knew the brutality of the storm we were driving into and honestly feared for our lives.

Temperatures still lingered around zero with raging winds blowing us all over the road. Blizzard conditions developed the further west we drove. Streaming crossways in front of our headlights, the snow grew heavier blinding our vision. Mom, terrified, pleaded with me to stop. Unwilling to relinquish control or jeopardize Easy Brick's welfare, it was my sheer determination that made us plough through the white out across Nebraska as we pushed towards the Rockies.

Twenty two hours later, exhausted and more than a little disoriented, we finally saw the lights of Denver. At three o'clock in the morning, the dark streets were deserted. We wound our way around town and finally found the Stock Grounds. Physically and mentally drained, we wandered through dimly lit barns looking for our stalls. Easy Brick was glad to be on solid ground and rolled in the fresh shavings after gulping down a bucket of water. Feeling confident the horse was taken care of, Mom and I finally headed to the hotel for some much needed rest.

The horse show held prior to the sale lasted four days. Rested, Easy Brick rallied quickly and we won the All-Around in our division. The promised chaps, the advertised prize for the award, were replaced by a disappointing cowboy *lamp* and perhaps portended the coming events. However, we unwittingly believed Easy's recent success at the show would add value translating to a higher bid in the sale ring, as it should have.

The day before the sale, we moved Easy Brick from the show barn to the sale barn. I posted a flyer on his door that bragged about his accomplishments, breeding and kind disposition. Recently won awards proudly displayed on his stall door conveyed his readiness to show and win for another owner.

The atmosphere in the sale barn was completely different than the show barn. Raucous unruly horses, many on their first trip away from the farm, wildly banged against the metal stalls. Big agents brought a slew of horses. They posted sale information on stall doors and tried to lure prospective buyers with candy set out in front of their fancy displays. Most horses were represented by some type of seller's agent who stood ready to show their stock and lay a line on anyone expressing an interest — no matter how remote.

Buyers came from all over the country. A few had been at the horse show, but most of the buyers came in only for the sale. They marked their sale books, refining their search to candidates who maintained promise and dismissed the horses not meeting their criteria. Easy and I rode in the demonstration alongside other sale horses giving the potential buyers an opportunity to view the prospects. Horses nervously gnashed their teeth, loped around on wrong leads, spooked and crashed into us. Protective, I did my best to keep Easy Brick away from the disruptive horses. I was certainly proud of our accomplishments and my horse, but I had an uneasy feeling and became increasingly leery and defensive.

Arriving the morning of the sale, Easy looked handsome, slick and shiny, just as happy to see me as he had been the day before. He greeted me hungrily, nickering at the sound of my voice, as clueless as I to the consequences of the day's event. Standing by the stall I answered questions from buyers. Many seemed surprised to find Easy Brick represented by his young owner, without the assistance of a grown up, trainer or seller's agent. But that is how it had always been; pals, together through thick and thin.

As our turn approached, a ring man came by and asked if there was a reserve on the sale of Easy. During our long drive, in need of a diversion from the treacherous roads, Mom and I discussed the sale price. We decided not to accept any bid below $7,500.00 — a substantial amount for a Quarter Horse gelding like Easy in 1979. Following directions, I told the man our reserve price.

The man then asked if I needed someone to *lead* Easy into the sale ring. The preposterous question struck me as strange. Puzzled, I said no. This guy obviously didn't know I had driven all the way from Wisconsin through blizzard conditions to get here. Ignorant to my resourcefulness, he did not know I prepared and showed Easy without the assistance of a trainer or agent. Certainly I could *lead* him into a sale ring.

Mom stayed with me for as long as she could bear. The sale barn was freezing and she was shivering from the cold. Sensing my apprehension, she left to warm up and watch the sale. Her departure also gave me room to grieve. Although it was my idea to sell Easy, it was still with mixed emotions. We had won many prizes, including my first belt buckle, learned more than I could tell and celebrated many good times together. Easy was my friend and suddenly I felt as if I was betraying his trust in me. How could I guarantee a good home through an auction? What if Easy's new owners were mean and treated him poorly?

Riotous noise from the sale arena brought me out of my trance. The auctioneer's rumbling voice played background to the banging of metal shoes striking steel stall walls. Intermixed with the shrill whinnying of nervous horses the noise was unnerving. The clamor was disrupted only by the deliberate sound of the hammer cracking the podium as it slammed down marking the end of bidding.

As our turn grew nearer, the volume escalated to a new level. Soon the ring man was shoving Easy and me into this minute, sawdust-covered 14' X 30' sale ring. The noise momentarily quieted while the auctioneer read Easy's resume. The man bragged about Easy Brick's quiet temperament as evidenced by this "little lady" from Wisconsin leading him, the auctioneer's words sounding condescending to my ears.

Then the roar began again! The sale pen was electric and sizzled with energy. But Easy Brick kept his cool as I led him back and forth in the tiny little area. The auctioneer's chanting droned on and while I knew he was saying something, I had no idea what. Deafened by the noise, I kept walking Easy in circles.

Suddenly, the gavel cracked down on the podium, silencing the racket. The arena grew quiet. Still, I did not know what was going on. I looked up to see the lighted board displaying the current bid, but it was directly overhead out of my view. Watching from the stands, Mom tried to get my attention but knew her efforts were futile. At this point in the sale, she had no way to communicate with me. While warming up in the sale arena, she had begun to understand how this auction thing worked.

In 1979 the U.S economy was diving headlong into its worst post-World War II recession. Mortgage rates were on the rise, job security was vulnerable and expensive hobbies like horse shows were threatened by a failing economy and rising inflation. Mom watched horse after horse come into the sale arena. Many had resumes better than Easy Brick's. Mares in foal to stallions with breeding fees in excess of $5000 were lucky to bring $3,500 in the sale arena. The market was down.

The action on Easy Brick elevated to the highest levels Mom had seen. In the previous twenty horses to sell, none had achieved this level of enthusiasm. Frustrated at her inability to get word to me to accept the bid, she tried in vain, but was simply too far away. Long before cell phones or beepers, she had no way to get the message to me. Powerless, she observed from afar. She watched as the auctioneer leaned over the podium and asked if I would accept the bid.

Confused, I had no idea where the bidding ended. *It was so loud.* I asked the auctioneer if the final bid reached $7,500. It had not. Mom and I agreed not to accept anything below

$7,500. Looking up to the auctioneer, I said emphatically, "No sale."

Leaving the arena, Easy Brick's ears went up. He too was happy to get out of that noisy place and be back at his hay bag in the corner of his stall. My head already hung low as Mom came into view. The look on her face told me all I needed to know. With equal parts disappointment and frustration, Mom delivered the bad news; bidding had ended at $7,300. Mom tried to reassure me — I had done exactly what we agreed to do — not accept a bid under $7,500. I had followed directions to the tee. But it was so close! I "no saled" a horse over a $200.00 shortfall.

As novices to auctions, we were without the foresight to have a secondary plan. Now the purpose of a ring man seemed clear as a bell. As a seller observing from the audience alongside buyers, $7300.00 was a home run. Had there been any way for Mom to regain control, to convey her conclusions to me, the *ring man*, she would have nodded her head. The auctioneer's words "SOLD for $7,300.00 to the gentleman in the....." would have completed the sale.

Mom and I would have driven home ecstatic. We would have laughed about the long arduous drive and the treacherous roads. The twenty hour trip from hell would have brought laughs later along with the loser all-around award now stuffed in the tack compartment. All of Mom's whining would have been worth it — had I just taken the last bid. Instead, the recurring payoff — that thing I had grown accustomed to receiving — was experience.

The drive home seemed longer than the treacherous trip out had been although it only took sixteen hours. Returning with an empty pocket and a horse in the trailer, the results of our trip were the exact opposite of my objective. Unable to fulfill my dreams of showing around the nation, I was broke, had a horse with no purpose and felt embarrassed over my naivety.

Blindly, I walked into something I knew nothing about. Never again would I enter an arena with so little knowledge of the strategy of the game.

As for Easy Brick, he was happy to return to his familiar home. He never did understand the implications of the sale. It was just another exhibition to him, one without a stop at the backdrop for a photo op.

Eventually I overcame the fallout from the sale. The importance of deciphering live bids from deluded illusions of grandeur had been made crystal clear. Reflecting later, Mom remembers me leaving the ring proudly after maturely uttering those words I would later regret. Who could imagine two little words could have such repercussions? They could never be retracted and would be the cause of much reflection in the months and years to come.

Forever more, whenever there was a sale, be it a horse, a house, a car or a contract, I would remember Easy Brick.

Words have meanings;

understand their implications before speaking them.

Easy Brick with Jennifer Lynn
Winning a showmanship class in 1979

Easy Brick became Jennifer's first real show horse. Together, Jennifer, Easy and I hit the road. Answering my calling, I launched my horse training career at age seventeen coaching Jennifer atop Easy Brick while I rode any horse I could get my hands on.

Easy Brick developed navicular disease, a debilitating bone disorder. He was later sold for $725.00 to another little girl whose father could not afford a more expensive horse. He undoubtedly did more than satisfy her dreams of owning a horse. May he rest in peace as he fulfilled more dreams than imaginable by a star struck teenager.

Photo Courtesy Waltenberry Photography

From top: Jennifer, Tom Davidson (Cindy's fiancé), Mom (Sally Lynn), Stephanie, Deb, Tana and Cindy at the WQHA State Show

Family to support me and
freedom to pursue my dreams
I had it all — truly a lucky girl!

Chapter 9

The Haves & the Have Nots

Nowhere is the discrepancy between the Haves and the Have Nots more prevalent than in the horse world. In any given class at any given show, equestrians compete together, theoretically on equal terms. In reality, one rider may be showing a $2500 horse as another sits on top of a $100,000 horse. It is not uncommon for a wealthy exhibitor to have spent more on her saddle than another exhibitor spent on his horse.

The Haves spend money keeping many shopkeepers in business while the Have Nots barter, trade and stitch their own designer show shirts. And while one group drives into the show grounds in a million dollar bus tricked out with marble counter tops, satellite television and the latest technology including air ride for all; the other might arrive in a ratty old farm truck pulling a borrowed horse trailer. However, when they enter the show arena, all are judged on equal terms.

Growing up in a nice middle class neighborhood in a conservative Midwestern town, we lived a quiet, comfortable life never going without. But in the world of horses, where people spend more on their horse's shoes than most spend outfitting their family, I was definitely a Have Not.

Easy Brick was the nicest horse the Lynn family had owned to date. Although his purchase price challenged my father's concept of reason, he was not an expensive horse. In retrospect, Little Billy had been a hell of a deal. Although Easy Brick did not come with a saddle, bridle or gold pad, he did share many of Little Billy's best attributes. Easy had the same big heart and kind nature but had the look of a fine show horse with a pretty head and correct confirmation. His movement, neither good nor bad, long nor short, made him more of an in-betweener. Easy Brick did not excel at either the English or the western but indeed, he gamely tried anything I asked of him. And, he was the horse I had.

A few friends had specialty horses bred to be especially good at one event or another. Many competitors spent considerably more than my parents had spent on Easy Brick. A few of the more ruthless competitors discarded any horse that could not immediately produce a win for them.

But supposedly the judges never know how much was paid for the horse you were sitting on, what kind of rig you pulled or how fancy the stall decorations were. The judges did not know what you wore the day before, if your horse wore matching monogrammed blankets or whether your boots were new or just newly polished. They did not know how many horses you owned or what kind of car your parents drove. What counted was how well you performed with the horse you were showing.

We all wanted the same thing: to win! And though I did not win all the time, I certainly won my share. There would always be competitors who could afford more than I could and those who won more than I did. And sometimes, those with the most expensive horses did win. But just as often, when times got tough, they quit, incapable of enduring the failure it takes to win.

Easy Brick was my guy and I loved him as only a kid could. I also loved to show in many events but had only one horse to compete with. Easy was a cheerful companion standing pretty in an early morning halter class and running hard at dusk in a barrel class vying for the All-Around award after a hard day of showing. He loaded for me every time as I learned to drive a trailer, always came to the stall with his ears up and would try just about anything for me. In return, I pampered him as much as possible, rubbing him down with liniment and wrapping his legs in poultice even if he didn't need it.

Catherine, a fellow competitor from an elite family, did not have to worry about wrapping her horse's legs. Her parents paid a trainer to do that menial work. Overindulged, Catherine did not haul her own horse, clip him, bath him or nurse him when he was sick. Catherine did not saddle her own horse, clean her tack, or even know what kind of bridle her horse wore. She was no horseman.

Without a work ethic, lacking the skills, desire and concern for the horse, Catherine didn't get it. Although she often fooled the judges with a perfectly turned out horse and state-of-art equipment, she couldn't fool the horse and when the going got tough she was left out, without the tools to handle a difficult situation on her own. Catherine's parents were too busy entertaining, making money or spending money to give Catherine the tools she needed to cope. She had no desire to learn or fit in; she just wanted the glory that came with a win.

Rebecca, also born in a privileged world, wanted to wrap her horse's legs. She knew how to properly prepare her horse, Jake, and desperately wanted to stay late, clip Jake's whiskers, wash his tail and give him his late night snack. She longed to be there first thing in the morning to feed him, clean his stall, turn him out and dust him off. Most of all, she yearned to rid herself of the constant shadow that followed her everywhere, protecting her from falls, false hopes and preventing her from fulfilling her dreams. But overprotective parents, fearful of retaliation against their life in the political arena, prevented

Rebecca's father from granting his only daughter, her only wish, freedom to fail. Her father could not afford that luxury, for he did love his daughter, too much to risk any fallout from his dog-eat-dog world of money and power.

It had taken a few years of growing up, of miles driven to fairgrounds far and near, of wanting more and longing for, but I discovered that I had it all — I was a Have, not a Have Not. I found I had something money could not buy, a passion that was not for sale and the freedom to pursue it.

The difference between the Haves and the Have Nots was not money or possessions. Haves foster passion that burns in their belly. They develop drive, find the fortitude to try and fail and try again, and maintain the conviction to get it right, at all cost. The Haves forfeit time, expend all their energy and spend hours drilling. Determination, strength and courage are characteristics of the Haves, not the Have Nots. Money had nothing to do with it. Later, my career would be built on the Haves. Some had money and some did not. But all had passion, courage and freedom to follow their dreams.

It occurred to me that people perceived as having it all may be the ones who have nothing at all. I did not have $7300.00 in my pocket after an auction, nor did I have a fancy rig or a $5000.00 saddle, but I still had my passion. The fire in my belly burned hotter and my enthusiastic devotion to this four-legged beast of burden grew stronger. For those who have a passion - something that drives them to wake early and stay up late, to try, fall down, then get up and try again — are truly the ones who have it all.

The affluent had a lot that money could buy.
But no price can be paid for freedom to develop
the passion it takes to become a winner.

Horse show family, assistant trainer Katie, Stephanie, Charlotte Berrier, Kerith Welch and Jill Martin

Definitely a group of haves —

some with money some without.

All of us had pride, purpose and passion.

**Stephanie, a serious student,
even at sixteen**

Unaware how to accomplish my goals,
all I wanted was to be a hand.

Chapter 10

Traditions

Becoming a horse trainer was not exactly a conscious decision. With two simple words, "NO SALE," I had failed to seize the opportunity to sell Easy Brick during the auction in Denver. With Easy Brick back home at my parents' Silvermine Farm, the time had come to make some decisions. Easy Brick had been a great horse for me. Together we won our first buckle, my first year-end hi-point and numerous other "first" awards. However, between his limited abilities and my limited funds, we were not going to be successful at a higher level. Ready for the challenge of tougher competition, this team needed shaking up.

Lacking the means to substitute Easy Brick with another horse of my own, I looked at my options. Smoke, my younger sister Jennifer's horse, had developed laminitis, a disease of the hoof. His unpredictable soundness made horse shows disappointing for Jennifer. She never knew if Smoke would be able to show until the morning of the horse show. Easy Brick would make a great step up horse for her. Meanwhile, a few people had asked me to ride or show their horses and some even offered to *pay* me!

With one foot out the door, yet still ensconced in my youth, I became an aspiring horse trainer at the age of seventeen. Jennifer, the youngest of the Lynn girls, was my first real student and Tiny Red Bay, a young English horse, my first official client-owned horse. Thinking I was quite unique; sure I knew more than most, I ventured into the open ring. A rebel to convention, attempting to prove my difference, I left conforming to others. Or so I thought.

Like teenagers throughout time, the easiest path to defy the establishment went through my closet. In the late 1970's, the accepted horse trainer's uniform started with Wrangler jeans and Roper boots. Wrangler made the only jeans specifically for cowboys, tough enough for five pounds of starch and long days in the saddle. Justin Ropers were a round toed, low heeled boot with an affordable price tag available in brown or, well, brown. Both were durable and practical and I wanted nothing to do with either.

Unique was my style of choice, not practicality. The last thing I wanted was to look like everyone else. Wearing Lee jeans tucked into tall boots, I felt too cool. However, only cutters sported this look and, to date, I had never cut a cow.

Dianne, the trainer from our neighboring state of Illinois, understood my zeal. From the moment I hit her radar, she recognized the intense desire and instinctually knew the success I craved. Dianne identified with the enterprising spirit, perceiving my innermost yearnings: to be respected by the great horsemen. The efforts to be different were not lost on Dianne either. However, it appeared to her my need to be different overshadowed my ability to ride a horse. Concluding a day would come when I could wear whatever brand of blue jean I wanted, she believed one day I could not only break the rules but write the rules.

Through a season of showing on the same circuit, Dianne made me realize that the people whose rules I wanted to break were the same people whose respect I sought. Her questions were never derogatory. Instead, she always asked the question knowing my answer would be the one she wanted. When questioning my tall boots, she would ask if my chaps fit over them or if I needed to change the boots prior to putting on my chaps to show. She wondered why I wore jeans that rode up my leg, or left the tail of my shirt un-tucked which prevented showing off the beautiful buckle I had won. In a horsemanship class, Dianne questioned my decision to put leg wraps on a horse when the horse did not spin fast. Although legal, the leg wraps led the judge to believe the horse spun hard. When the horse did not spin fast, the splint boots or wraps drew negative attention, potentially affecting the rider's score unfavorably.

Dianne questioned many of my choices always leading me to the conclusion she wanted me to discover on my own. If I wanted to be a professional, I had to look, dress and act as a professional. Dianne encouraged me to behave as if I already had the status that I so strongly desired. Always taught to respect my elders, I had never thought of the other trainers as my elders. I sincerely sought their approval, wanting nothing more than to be known as a *hand*: an exceptional horseman. I desperately wanted to be regarded as someone who was one with the horse, an extraordinary communicator, able to get along with and advance a horse's capacity to learn.

The trainers, whose dress code I rejected, were the very trainers whose respect I yearned for. By snubbing their dress code, I channeled attention to the wrong areas. The attention received by being different drew the wrong kind of notice. The trainers treated my unusual dress as juvenile and perceived me as amateurish — the very last thing I wanted. Acceptance from these seasoned professionals required understanding where they had come from.

Professional trainers had once been young, broke with tradition, blazed trails and developed better methods.

Cultivating superior practices for horsemen, they rolled carbon steel to fabricate sweet iron bits, concocted tinctures to heal wounds and melted steel to forge the perfect shoe. They founded associations creating a breed registry to bring recognition to their trade. They worked tirelessly, facilitating the business of training horses.

And yes, they designed hardware like jeans for riders that did not ride up your leg rubbing your knees raw, stood up to piles of dirt, hours in the sun and thousands of washings. They designed a comfortable boot to hold a spur, made it affordable and ensured it would quickly come free from a stirrup when danger approached.

While Wranglers and Ropers were the result of much trial and error, respecting the dress code of the pros meant more than wearing a uniform. While my heroes would have had fun laughing at my wardrobe malfunctions, they would much rather cheer my success watching me embrace their hard fought traditions.

As I hauled my little sister and her new horse, Easy Brick, around with my newly acquired client's horse, Tiny Red Bay, I began to emulate those who went before me. Acknowledging traditions of the successful forerunners seemed only right. With new found dignity, I put on a pair of Wranglers. But I never did own a pair of Ropers.

Easy Brick and Stephanie at a show in 1978
Together we were alone on the road.

Traditions are time honored customs
entrusted to those worthy of their merit.
If you are lucky enough to be entrusted,
Respect them.

Red as he was unloaded from the trailer in 1980

Skinny and wormy, my $1,200 project horse
was not much to look at. Who could predict he
would be the catalyst to launch a career that provided
a lifetime of fulfillment.

Opportunity exists everywhere,
in the strangest of places, oddest settings and
in the least likely scenarios.

Chapter 11

Opportunity

A year out of high school and desperate to prove I could make money in the horse business, I bought a young prospect. He was a two year old gelding I called Red. A big red sorrel with a kind eye and gentle character, he showed promise as a show horse.

Attending the University of Wisconsin in Eau Claire, I floundered in classes ranging from Art History to geology. Like a ship without a sail, I took classes with appealing names wandering through the class list with no intended destination. I lived at home with my parents and continued to work at Silvermine Farm, our family farm. My parents purchased the horse property as an investment in 1978. The property sat on 80 acres west of our home in Eau Claire and consisted of an old farmhouse, hay barns, a large horse barn, as well as pastures and indoor and outdoor arenas.

Even after the renovations, the project kept my mother, Sally, busy dealing with farmers, tractors, co-ops, broken equipment and trying to find stall cleaners — a never ending job nearly impossible to fill in west central Wisconsin. Taking interest in the business, I cleaned stalls, fed, trained a few horses and generally helped out. Still just a kid in my parents' eyes, my ideas were summarily dismissed. My participation in stall cleaning was, however, expected in return for the opportunities ₛes. Hoping to move more than manure, I set ₐspiring to be a successful professional horseman.

₍ as a project horse, was my ticket off campus and ₐₐ I dreamt of. All I wanted to do was ride horses. ₘcluded putting a few months training into Red and ₛₑ. ₐm for a profit. Unfortunately, just after bringing him to Silvermine Farm, he suffered a serious injury to his leg. Red severed the tendon that ran behind his pastern while turned out in a pasture. Vital in shock absorption, the pastern is located between the hoof and fetlock joint. Slender, shapely yet incredibly strong, the pastern is the bearer of thousands of pounds of pressure imposed during the million steps taken throughout a horse's lifetime. It is the part of the leg that absorbs the relentless concussive force of the footfall with each step the horse takes.

The injury was in a difficult place to treat and required 30 days of stall rest. The pastern and ankle were bandaged, stabilized and required at least six months in a special shoe. The farrier hand forged the shoe, welding it to make a lift at the heel. The rise in the heel maintained pressure on both ends of the tendon encouraging its re-growth. The funky shoe looked like *Jane Jetson's* high heel, cost five times more than the fanciest shoe in my mother's closet and had to be replaced every four weeks!

My first lesson should have been that making money in the horse business was not going to be as easy as previously thought. Not to be put off, I doctored, hand walked, and eventually put Red back in full training. Twelve months behind schedule, I finally advertised Red for sale. I placed an ad in a local Tri-State horse paper and hoped for the best. In due course, a prospective buyer called and set up an appointment for her trainer to come look at Red. As the appointed day drew near, I clipped Red's whiskers, legs and bridle path; washed and braided his mane and tail; primped and fussed over him until he glistened like a new penny. Red radiated good health.

Proud of my little project horse, I anxiously awaited the arrival of the prospective buyer's trainer. It had been a long eighteen months of caring for Red. The countless hours spent fretting, soaking legs in Epsom salts, changing bandages, hand walking, tending to wounds resulting from the bandages intended to heal, and ultimately, riding and training, did not prepare me for the trainer who walked through the barn doors that fateful day.

Her name was Lynn Salvatori Palm and, in 1982, she was the leading trainer in the English division of the American Quarter Horse Association. She had won six of the nine three year old English Stakes classes ever to be held at the Quarter Horse Congress in Ohio. Surprised, and with some trepidation, I brought Red out for Lynn's inspection. Compared to Lynn and all of her accomplishments, Red and I seemed insignificant, of little consequence. Yet whatever apprehension I felt disappeared once I tacked up Red and started to ride. Red went right to work performing like a well oiled machine. My job had been to educate, train, and present Red to the best of his abilities. For a year and a half we prepared for this day. Lynn watched with a critical eye while I earnestly awaited her appraisal. Lynn's job was to determine if Red seemed compatible with her customer's needs and Lynn scrutinized our every move, analyzing Red's capabilities. Her probing questions seemed to revolve only around Red's preparation and training. Now we waited for judgment to be passed down by the expert.

When she said goodbye I was sure that would be the last I would hear from the legendary trainer. Red had been a good boy, but we were country bumpkins in this jet-setting trainer's world of winners. Returning home from school the next day, Mom surprised me by saying Lynn called with a few questions.

Assuming her questions would be regarding the soundness or prognosis of Red, she shocked me again by offering me a job. Lynn needed an apprentice and hoped I would be interested in filling her vacancy. Ecstatic, I didn't give it a second thought. After finishing the semester and contrary to my father's wishes, I packed a few belongings and moved to the U.P of Michigan.

Nestled between the ski slopes it is best known for, Bessemer is a tiny town just over the Wisconsin border, south of Lake Superior. It sits between the resort slopes of Big Powderhorn Mountain, Blackjack and Indianhead. Bessemer rests on the edge of the Gogebic range, home to the speculative mining craze of the late 1800's — the last place on earth you would expect a trainer of Lynn's significance to settle. Lynn lived with her husband, Peter, at the base of Powderhorn Mountain in a ski chalet and leased a barn a few miles from the chalet. The remote and obscure location became my home for two years.

The work was hard, the hours were long. It was often dirty, mostly grueling, always challenging; and the most enlightening experience of my young life. Lynn introduced me to a level of showing I had previously only dreamt of or read about. We traveled across the country with the horses. I drove the truck and trailer while she flew in to meet us wherever we were showing. As her trust in me grew so too did the responsibilities she bestowed. Soon I was riding, preparing and showing her best clients' horses. In no time, she introduced me to the major players as her protégé.

The experience shaped my career and who I have become in my pursuits. In the twenty two months I lived in the frozen U.P., I discovered more about who I did and did not want to be than I had in my previous 22 years. I am grateful for all the lessons learned and the opportunity to have the connection with Lynn.

No one could have prepared me for the opportunity that presented itself that day back at Silvermine Farm. I can only, once again, be grateful to have been raised by parents who taught me to always do my best and for the strong foundation they, along with Murph and many others, provided. Murph taught us to care about the horse first and to give the horse credit for success and take responsibility for all mistakes. Most importantly, he taught us to take care of business, be the best we can be, that if we are good horsemen first, we will be rewarded for our efforts.

Trophies are not given for arrogance or self importance. Honor is the result of hard work, honesty and diligence. Lynn and I both knew the limits of my horse that day. No matter how famous she was, Red's preparation had been thorough and Lynn recognized that too. Lynn's customer ended up buying Red and they had a successful run at the horse shows. Red's new owner became a friend of mine and is currently training horses in Wisconsin.

Opportunities present themselves each and every day.
Misfortune provides just as many
opportunities as good fortune.
Determining the outcome is a personal choice.

Photo Courtesy Waltenberry Photography

Laura (Strebel) Sheedy with Red Badger Prince
Turned Out — a pretty pair and
opportunities abounded for everyone

Photo courtesy Lynn Palm

Lynn Palm at her best, instructing a student.

To this day, Lynn makes no excuses for her expectations. The demands she places on others are no less than she demands of herself.

Chapter 12
Demand Excellence

In 1982 at the age twenty, I finished spring semester at the university, packed my gear (mostly show clothes and cowboy boots) and moved to Bessemer, Michigan. Convinced I had indentured myself to a lifetime of "grunt" work, my father argued against the move. He feared my life would consist of nothing but the intense manual labor that surrounded the senseless animal I loved. He considered horses to be expensive recyclers of money to manure. Mel Lynn did not want his number three daughter subjected to the heavy physical work nor did he want me associated with the likes of a bunch of cowboys. As all fathers want for their daughters, mine wanted all of his daughters to go to college and become entrepreneurs in the "real" business world. The last thing he wanted was for one of his daughters to be enwrapped in the circus-like world of horse showing. He worried the lifestyle would not produce stability and fiercely protested my decision to move to Bessemer.

Dad lost the fight but won the argument. The physical demands of the job were considerable; comparable to hard labor. At the beck and call of the boss, I lived in her house under her rule. Each day started with chores of feeding, watering, turning out horses, cleaning stalls, grooming then saddling horses for Lynn to ride. At first I could not brush a horse suitably, saddle one quick enough or wrap a longe line correctly. Tired and a little homesick, I wondered why I had been hired if my skills were indeed so inept.

Lynn demanded excellence and made no excuses for asking for the best from everyone. She did nothing without a purpose. Every move she made had a specific and intended goal. At first, I did not get it. She simply seemed like an eccentric woman with a control issue. Everything had to be just so or she would explode with anger — her annoyance over any incompetence obvious in her tone and manner. Every bridle had to be cleaned and hung precisely each and every time. Every brush had to be put in the brush cart, right side up, in its proper slot after each use, no matter how soon you were going to use it again. She paid meticulous attention to detail and allowed no hair to be out of place, no scratch to be unattended, no piece of shavings left in the alleyway. Even if *she* left the grooming area with hoof pickings on the floor, a brush on a rail or a bridle unkempt on a hook, she angered at my allowing it.

Luckily Lynn's brisk business provided *numerous* opportunities every day to learn how to properly put bridles away (neatly wrapped after cleaning with oil); pick every stall clean expeditiously and hang a longe line with exact precision *each and every* time immediately after its use. Lynn, a perfectionist, could bark orders, ridicule with a scorn then applaud my efforts with just enough approval to make me come back for more. Some days with survival uncertain, I questioned my decision to work for this hard driving woman. Then a new day would dawn, the routine would start anew and I would try again to satisfy the master as well as my personal appetite for success.

Our working routine commenced; an eagerness to please along with my own adolescent ideals drove me to seek Lynn's approval. Slogging through the debris, persevering in order to sit on her horses, I took whatever morsels came my way. Lynn began to trust my understanding of her expectations and passed off more responsibilities to me. With every additional task, the bell on the alarm clock rang earlier. Finishing morning chores promptly ensured my availability to ride with Lynn whenever the opportunity presented itself. Eventually she delegated specific horses for me to ride without her presence and I made every effort to exceed her expectations.

Under her watchful eye, I took the criticism, survived the angry outbursts of disappointment and endured my life as the occasional whipping post. Each day I tried desperately to advance the horses further than Lynn expected, struggling to prove my value as a horse trainer. When Lynn rode a horse I worked with, I wanted it to perform with greater skill than she thought possible; the desire to prove my abilities exceeded only by my perseverance.

No matter the results of a training session with Lynn, I always wanted more; more instruction, more responsibility, more horses to ride and more time to get it right. And always I got more; more work, more criticism and more reason to get it right. Her review, however disparaging, always came with a side of encouragement. Sometimes, Lynn delivered the promise of hope; all sins of failure pardoned, Lynn never gave up on potential. She asked, *demanded*, the best in everyone around her. She built her career, an extremely successful career, on the expectation that everyone could give a little more, try a little harder, *be* a little better. And so I tried, even as it seemed nothing could be done to please this demanding woman.

Fortunately, there were the horses. They always needed me, often were glad to see me and offered much needed comfort to my weary soul. With much of Lynn's time spent on the details of running her business, she rarely got to the barn before I finished morning chores. Lynn appointed Gaucho, a young gelding she owned, to be in my string of daily rides. Horse trainers can rarely afford to justify spending their limited time on horses they own. It is probably the one ambition shared by all horse trainers; to be able to train, ride and show horses they own exclusively, eliminating wants, wishes and deadlines made by owners who may know nothing about horses. Fortunately for me, Lynn did not have time to ride her own horses.

Gaucho had a good mind, an easy gait and more than a little talent. I enjoyed riding him and he became my post teenage "Little Billy" — a companion to fill a lonesome void. Lynn laid out a very specific exercise plan for Gaucho and me. Because he was the one horse I knew I could ride every day without Lynn, I often rode him before she made it to the barn. Since she did not see me ride him regularly, Lynn instead questioned our progress and offered ideas on how to further his development. Lynn made a point to watch me school Gaucho every once in a while and after each session, her words were a variation of the same message: keep doing what you are doing. Certain with each successive ride Gaucho had improved enough to move on, my frustration deepened. Convinced the horse was capable of progressing to the next level, I craved the approval to advance.

It felt like Cricket all over again. But now, my almost adult head, made me question Lynn's intentions. Was she holding me back because she did not think I was good enough? Becoming discouraged, disappointment took hold and made me wonder if I had what it took. Long days with little reward took their toll on my psyche. Lynn, always positive even when angry, treated me the same every day — oblivious to my frustrations or my moods.

One sunny afternoon after a long day of work, we took Gaucho and another young horse out for a drive. We hitched each horse to an old fashioned two wheeled buggy, jumped in the cart behind them and drove out the driveway. We crossed the railroad track where Gaucho spooked nearly tipping the cart over on top of himself. We drove through a field on an old tractor lane, everyone enjoying the beautiful day. Clueless as to our destination, Gaucho and I trailed behind Lynn, happy to be off the farm.

We ended up at a local tavern with an old hitching post out front. I stayed with the horses while Lynn went inside. She came out of the tavern with the owners and cold beer for each of us. We drank our beer; Lynn shared a few laughs with her friends, then we drove the horses back through the countryside to the barn where Lynn promptly left me to do evening chores. Her departure did not bother me not a bit, it had been the most fun I had been allowed to have since my arrival.

The next day, Lynn arrived early giving me directions for the morning along with two lists. She was leaving the following day for a big show in Berrien Springs, Michigan, and needed the specific items on her list packed in the horse trailer. The second sheet listed the horses' names that needed to be clipped, bathed and blanketed. Breezing into the makeshift office, she instructed me to saddle Gaucho with her saddle and put the saddle I used on Blue, a well schooled accomplished show horse. Taking her directions without question, I inwardly prepared for a chiding – this would be the first time Lynn rode Gaucho in over a month.

After warming up a few minutes, Lynn, sitting on Gaucho, stopped in the center of the arena and began directing me with Blue. She asked if I had ever changed leads and inquired about my experience with lead changes, a complex maneuver requiring exact timing and a precise feel. Although I knew how to change leads, my fear of censure led me to downplay my knowledge. Lynn surprised me by walking me through her routine for changing leads. The preliminary steps sounded woefully familiar. The exercises were identical to those I had begrudgingly spent the previous weeks practicing with Gaucho.

Making every effort to accurately do as she instructed, I loped off. The results were exactly what Lynn expected and I wanted. Blue changed leads effortlessly as directed back and forth from his right lead to his left lead and back again to his right lead. Blue was a great teacher, highly trained and a willing partner. Satisfied with the accomplishment, outwardly smiling and inwardly relieved, I let Blue take a break.

Lynn told me to keep an eye on her and Gaucho while I walked and cooled down Blue. She cantered off and took Gaucho through the same paces she had just asked me to do with Blue. Then, without forewarning, Lynn asked Gaucho to change from his left lead to his right lead. He completed the lead change as if the pair had been changing leads under saddle forever! Amazed, I watched with admiration. Lynn's ability to achieve this level of cooperation from Gaucho seemed unreal. She had not ridden Gaucho in several weeks, yet she stepped on and, in ten minutes, had him changing leads. It was remarkable to watch.

After getting a couple of changes each direction, Lynn stopped Gaucho and rubbed the sweet spot on his neck under his mane. Admiring her talent, I spoke in awe, her ability to guide Gaucho so willingly seemed incredible. Lynn just laughed and patted me on the back. But there was no swagger in her step, no "awe shucks" in her air.

"I don't know why you are so surprised," she said. "You did all the work. Gaucho wouldn't have changed leads if you hadn't laid the ground work."

Dumbfounded at her acknowledgement, I tied Blue up in his stall and began to remove his tack. Lynn, in a nearby stall doing the same with Gaucho, detailed the work she expected from me in her absence. After Lynn returned, we would continue the training of Gaucho's lead changes. For now, it was back to the basics for Gaucho and me.

As I un-wrapped Gaucho's legs, Lynn worked a brush over him and explained her concern over my inexperience as well as my newness to her program. She articulated her need to be the first person to actually *ask* for the flying lead change while on Gaucho. Lynn justified her decision by recounting all of the naughty responses the first attempts can bring about from a horse.

We laughed over her stories about horses kicking out, running off and throwing their heads, reins breaking as the horse leapt to one side or another or being kicked out of the saddle after the horse bucked through a lead change. She assured me, with the next horse we trained for lead changes, she would let me be the first to actually ask for the change. She finished her work at the barn and left me to finish mine. That day, another fourteen hour marathon, ended with exhaustion. A great day, I felt as if I had been initiated into Lynn's program.

While some of Lynn's ways seemed borne of trivial means, there was always a method to her madness. It is from my long fruitful days under Lynn's employ that I learned to have, follow and analyze goals; to accomplish those goals by establishing a plan. I discovered the importance of paying attention to every single detail, no matter how small; to consider all aspects of a plan and carefully adjust goals along the way. Lynn taught me to stop and take a breath when I got lost; to use my head to figure out where my path had gone astray. Working with her, I matured from a young passionate girl to a professional intent on honing my skills and becoming the best horse trainer I could be. Now, my own signature wrap identifies my longe line when left out of place at a horse show.

My customers may think that I, too, am an eccentric woman with control issues. So be it. I am forever grateful that Lynn never felt compelled to apologize for demanding excellence in those around her. Through the long arduous days spent at Royal Palm Ranch I learned again, as from Murph, that we learn the most from those who expect the most.

> *Expect nothing from others and you will never be disappointed;*
> *expect nothing from yourself, and you will never be satisfied.*
> *Excellence results from refusing to surrender high expectations,*
> *no matter the obstacles that appear on your path.*

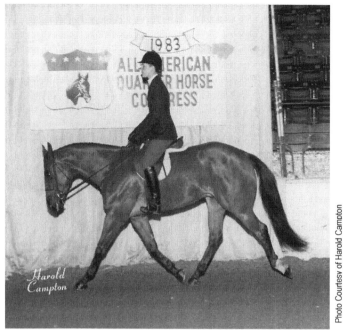

Photo Courtesy of Harold Campton

**Stephanie on Gaucho at the 1983 All-American Quarter Horse Congress
Three-year-old Hunter Under Saddle Stakes Class**

Making the finals on Gaucho more than exceeded my expectations. For Lynn, the resulting sale accomplished her goal.

**Stephanie, still smiling, outside Lynn's barn on
another gray November day**

Daylight-shortened days made the work days seem longer as did
the never-ending gray and endless work load that surrounds the
horses. While often frustrated, there were always the horses,
reason for laughter and the promise of light that always shone
brightly.

For one step ahead lay the doors that opened to a world
previously unknown. There were doors to arenas yet to be
claimed, adventures still to embark upon and so much
knowledge yet to be gained, just through those doors.

Chapter 13
Perseverance

Two days after the initiating ride on Gaucho, Lynn called from Berrien Springs, Michigan. Midsummer, it had been a particularly grueling few weeks and Lynn's absence following my breakthrough ride afforded much needed time alone to reflect and contemplate. But the separation was short lived. The show, the most prestigious of the summer, was huge and Lynn had her hands full. Limited to the number of horses she could show, Lynn needed help. With more work than she anticipated, she flew me in to help prepare the horses *and* to show the "slack" — the extra horses she could not show. Driving into the Berrien Springs show grounds after the small aircraft dropped me like a sack of mail, I took in the scene.

People and horses were scattered everywhere around the lush county fairgrounds. Grooms led horses back and forth from stables to arenas; trainer's schooled students and horses while exhibitors showed in one of the show arenas. We drove between freshly painted arenas on one side and barns on the other. As we passed the different barns, I read the names advertised boldly outside stalls elaborately decorated for the event. Color coordinated curtains covered the plain brown wooden stall walls. Ribbons, evidence of their success in the show ring, hung proudly above tack trunks and tables set with matching chairs and décor. Pots brimmed with bright colorful flowers making the plain barns appear quite dignified. The decorations turned the bare barns into a festive Mecca for Quarter Horse enthusiasts.

The event was clearly well attended. Stall curtains revealed names of trainers from all parts of the country. They came from New York, Texas, Florida, Arizona, Montana and all parts in between. The names were those I had previously only seen in magazines, heard about through the grapevine or idolized from afar. Looking around, the scene inspired awe; mixed emotions of respect, wonder, reverence and definitely a good dose of intimidation.

Lynn introduced me to all of the venerable big wigs, her peers, as her assistant. The introduction opened the door to a new world. I felt an immediate acceptance; the result of the association with Lynn and part of something much larger than I. The feeling changed my perception of the past month's efforts. The long days of endless frustration suddenly seemed a lifetime ago. As a competitor, the show introduced me to an entirely different level of competition; one that previously only occupied my dreams. I don't remember the show for me specifically — Lynn always won — and I think my name was called out somewhere along the line. The magnitude of the scene vastly broadened my outlook; the prospects fueling the fire within.

Driving the horses home with Lynn enlightened me further. Spending 500 miles alone in a truck with nothing to do but talk, you learn a good deal about a person. Plans for horses, shows and their marketing were discussed, dissected and parceled out. Switching from the passenger to the driver's seat, I thought the drive would be the first of many we undertook together. But as luck would have it, our traveling roles reversed through the coming show season. Lynn began flying into the horse shows and I became the truck driver.

Sometimes Lynn acted as the front man flying into the grounds in advance to set up stalls. Other times I arrived with the horses, arranged stalls, horses and tack so they were ready when she arrived. Lynn would fly in following a clinic she presented somewhere around the country or after showing for some prominent owner/trainer where she partnered in making champions. I continued to show her second string when available, but more importantly; she entrusted me to ride *every* horse at home. While she was crowning Super Horses, Congress and World Champions, I experimented with her methods, mimicked her routine, tried her techniques for myself, failed in the face of everyone and figured it out in solitude. All the while, the passion burned hotter.

Before being flown into the horse show at Berrien Springs, my job in Bessemer seemed like one of survival. My pride too great, I could not succumb to the pressure and return to school in the fall as my father wished. Although the job seemed to suck the energy out of me, I could not give up. Lynn drove everyone hard, herself included. She seemed to have endless energy, strength and stamina, expecting everyone around her to keep up her pace. Work days stretched into work weeks blurring the line between work time and down time. There seemed to be *no* time that Lynn did not work.

The induction into her program elevated my confidence, my goals and my inspiration. Horses, always my passion, now became my life, my obsession. Like an addict, I could not wait to get my next fix. Every loss presented an opportunity to learn; every win raised the bar exacting a new objective. Each new horse that came into the barn led to fresh aspirations, goals yet to be attained. Each rider who came to learn presented an opportunity to exceed Lynn's capacity to teach.

The thrill obtained from hearing your name called out amongst the most respected in the field is indescribable. Nothing else matters — getting to the horse show attempting to prove your valor once or one more time — fulfilling destiny in the riding arena the only worthy ambition.

My father was right about a lot of things. In the eyes of many, my life has been spent doing so called "grunt work." Horse trainers are perceived as nothing but the hired help to some - the work unfit for the elitist. The difficult and physically demanding work surrounding horses is never-ending. By their very nature, horses are time-consuming, destructive, needy and labor intensive. They make demands on your life, complicating simple holiday meals with upset stomachs of their own, interrupting nighttime dreams with a kick through the stall wall and enjoying a roll in freshly laid manure just before they are expected to enter the show ring. Through it all, the horsemen fight to fulfill their dreams of glory, finding satisfaction in the simple rewards the horses dole out – no matter how small the dose. Those who do not give into the exhaustion are rewarded with more than just trophies and ribbons. The enjoyment brought by a successful ride, one in which the rider's desires are understood by the animal under the saddle, are a reward beyond measure.

Achieving a goal takes perseverance. We do not start out in this life as the fastest, smartest, or best at anything. It is only through trial and error that we learn to succeed. After steady continual action, over as long a period as it takes, despite the difficulties and setbacks', reaching the end is often the best reward; accolades just a bonus for having finished with grace to the end. For my dad, I believe in his heart, he was proud I persevered, learned from the trials and tribulations of my youthful yearnings and became an entrepreneur, albeit in an industry he did not condone.

Photo Courtesy of Harold Campton

**Stephanie showing a Wild And Crazy Guy at the 1983 AQHA World
Championship Show in Junior Hunter Under Saddle**

Eventually trusted by Lynn to show her best client's horse at
our most prestigious event was the best prize I could have
received. The long hours, long forgotten, were replaced by a
sense of pride and self-respect: a feeling of belonging to this
group of "*hands*" I so longed to emulate.

*Success is not for the faint of heart:
it follows persistence to
those who remain undaunted by adversity.*

Stephanie & Laurel (Raether) Champlin
WQHQ State Show 1983

Leaning on each other,
we had each other's backs.
A bond built on shared hardships
would never be splintered.

Chapter 14

Trusted Friends

Friends come when you least expect them and often when you need them most. On an early December morning during my first winter in Bessemer, I awoke in a panic. Lynn, away at a show, left me in charge and I could tell by the bright light streaming in the windows, I had overslept. Lynn insisted we maintain a strict feeding schedule. Horses were fed at 6:30 in the morning and 5:00 in the evenings – without exception. In December, it did not begin to get light until 8:00 AM. Judging by the bright light, it was well past that and it took at least ten minutes to drive to the barn.

Lynn would be furious when she found out how late I was. Jumping out of bed, I noticed a note pinned to the door of my bedroom in Lynn's ski chalet. Following the directions on the note, I called Lynn's husband, Peter. Laughing, he asked if I had looked outside. I peered out the window to see my Pinto, the four wheeled version with a gas fed engine, buried under a foot of unmovable snow. After turning off my alarm clock, Peter had called the stable owner to alert him that I would not be able to get to the barn to feed the horses.

Lynn leased a barn eight miles from the base of the Powderhorn Mountain ski chalet she shared with her husband. Peter managed the lodging association and worked out of an office about a mile from their house. The stable owner lived on the property next to the stable and agreed to feed the horses on the rare occasions we were unable to be there. This situation certainly qualified as an emergency and Peter assured me the stable owner had been contacted and the horses fed. He would drive me to the barn after I got to his office.

Layering long underwear, jeans, turtleneck, and sweaters under my coveralls, I threw on my hat and gloves and put on my cross country ski shoes. When I stepped outside the air held the conspicuous quiet of a fresh snow. The bindings snapped closed breaking the hollow quiet like a gunshot when I stepped into my skis. I couldn't help but marvel at the pristine view. Looking at the ski mountain covered in fresh powder, I took a big breath letting the cold crisp air fill my lungs. Feeling close to Mother Nature, I noiselessly skied to Peter's office enjoying the novel mode of transportation.

At Peter's office, we loaded up his four-wheel drive with shovels, sand bags, chains and a two-way radio. Ready for an adventure, Peter dropped the snow plow on the front of the Scout and put the jeep in gear. Thirty minutes later, we arrived at the barn after plowing a passable route. We were met at the door by the frenzied calls of hungry horses. The owner had obviously not yet fed nor watered the horses and by now it was late morning. Peter angered at the incompetent owner's lack of responsibility. He helped me do chores then we plowed our way to lunch.

When Lynn returned, she was indeed furious — but not at me. Missing a feeding was inexcusable. Stalled horses must be kept to a very strict feeding schedule or they risk becoming colicky and sick. Irate after hearing about the missed feeding, Lynn met with the unreliable owner. The conversation did not go well. Three days later, we were hustling to find another barn.

Lynn owned 200 acres bordering the Gogebic National Forest ten miles from Lake Superior and planned to build her own facility in the frozen Upper Peninsula. However, not a stake had been laid, and this was December in Bessemer, Michigan. While the fourteen inches of snow stopped me and my Pinto in our tracks, it was a dusting compared to the annual 200 inches of snowfall expected every winter. Finding a suitable facility for Lynn's training horses in Bessemer was like finding water in the middle of the Sahara. There were no options. She lived in an extremely remote and impoverished area of the iron ridge. Few people lived there and even fewer were affluent enough to have a facility suitable for a world class trainer such as Lynn.

Lynn's show schedule took us to Florida for January but we would need somewhere to take the horses upon our return. After bringing in the New Year showing in West Palm Beach, we returned to the great white north late in January of 1983 and took the horses to my parents' place in Wisconsin, three hours southwest of Bessemer. Lynn went home to monitor the building of her new facility and traveled back and forth between Eau Claire and Bessemer for three months. While Lynn commuted, I stayed at home driving to Silvermine Farm everyday to ride the training horses.

Lynn's business had been stymied by the limited stabling at the leased barn. It did not take long for word to get out about the new show barn Lynn was building. She filled every stall before they were even built and had a waiting list for new clients. Her new facility would have twelve permanent stalls in the main barn, and room for additional temporary stalls for students in the 80' X 200' indoor arena. Not privy to all her goals, conversations or objectives, I expressed concern over the amount of work the additional horses would require.

It appeared that we – I – would need more help. Every mouth to feed meant another stall to clean, water bucket to fill, body to be groomed and mind to be trained. Just thinking about the extra work wore me out. In addition to the extra horses, Lynn planned four, week-long clinics where riders would come with their horses for intense instruction with Lynn. We had barn help in the year since I arrived, but no one lasted more than a few weeks. So it was with relief that I greeted the news of a new employee. Lynn's announcement calmed my fears — until I met her.

Returning home after a long April day of riding and hauling horses, I was beat. Winter in the U.P. had been kind allowing the construction of Lynn's new facility to be ahead of schedule. Although not complete, the new barn was finished enough to move horses into stalls. After riding, I took a load of horses to the new place. Well after midnight when I finally finished and got to my parents' house, all I wanted to do was climb into my own bed and sleep. Mom stood in the kitchen awaiting my arrival, something she'd stopped doing years ago. She reminded me we had a house guest; Lynn's new employee had arrived from Arizona. With all of the craziness, I had forgotten the girl was coming.

Not wanting to wake her, I let the filtered light from the bathroom guide me as I peeked into the bedroom. Suddenly a head of blonde curly hair popped up from the pillow on *my* bed!

Speaking quietly, Laurel introduced herself. Her softly accented voice brimmed with excitement even at this late hour. Sitting up, she began the tale of her beginnings working for an illustrious Arizona trainer. Suddenly I recalled the *glowing* recommendation that preceded this eager girl's arrival. Laurel, now wide awake, exhausted me further chattering on with obvious admiration for Lynn. Perfect — another Lynn Palm "groupie" I thought to myself. I stared at her, unable to believe that at midnight her blonde hair held a perfect curl. I rolled my eyes, shook sawdust from my hair and crawled into the bed parallel to mine. Thoughts of the rude awakening in store for Miss Laurel carried me off to a peaceful sleep.

The next morning, her hair still perfect, we dressed for the day ahead while Laurel continued her story. I waited while Laurel applied makeup I knew no one would see. As she snapped her fancy cosmetic case closed, she made an offhand comment about Lynn not granting us too much freedom. Now there's an understatement, I thought to myself. Maybe this sunny girl from Arizona would be okay.

Laurel and I each drove a truck and a trailer taking the last of the horses to Lynn's new facility. We arrived at "*Royal Palm Ranch*" mid day and dug in. The horses were unloaded and shuffled around to find stalls with suitable stable mates (neighbors who would not kick and fight with each other). Then we began the enormous task of unpacking and finding a place for all of the tack that had been stored in the horse trailer for five months. At first Laurel and I stumbled over each other, the misplaced tack, and the unfamiliarity. The nature of the task at hand made us work closely together and gave us an opportunity to feel each other out.

Laurel and I moved into our own ski chalet — a perk that came with the new girl. I moved out of Lynn's spare room and into the lower unit of the double apartment. At first Lynn wanted us to drive back and forth to the barn together. The arrangement gave us a chance to talk about something besides work. Laurel was surprised there were no 7-11s to get her morning Dr. Pepper or Dunkin' Donuts for coffee. Nope, no 7-11's, no convenience stores, no fast food, no *chain restaurants*, no yuppies — Bessemer was a long way from Scottsdale!

Laurel and I commiserated over the long days, the heavy work load and an endless to-do list. Laurel rolled her eyes and questioned her need to withstand the remedial lessons. But within a few weeks, she too learned the correct way to longe a horse, hang a longe line, roll a hose, clean tack and the many other precise methods Lynn required us to use. During my first year with Lynn, I had grown accustomed to Lynn's demands.

However, the pressure to perform made my high strung co-worker a bit anxious.

Laurel fretted whenever Lynn returned from a trip. At this point, considering myself a Lynn Salvatori Palm veteran, I had a few things figured out. Lynn, an absolute perfectionist, lived by a strict code, a highly regimented routine and an organized life. She remembered, in concise detail, exactly how she left things and despised discovering anything out of place, including her employees not picking up after her.

Upon Lynn's return from any trip, tired and perhaps overwhelmed with the unfinished work that lay ahead, she could not tolerate disorder. When she walked into the barn, wired and wiped out, her eyes focused on any detail out of place. It is a syndrome I valiantly, *and without success,* tried to overcome later in my own barn. Because you were away, everyone at home assumes you were on vacation. In truth, the work on the road is often ten times more exhausting than the work at home, making it vital to have harmony at home. You come home completely drained from travel yet hyper energized with fresh ideas along with their accompanying to do list. Any scrap out of place provokes anger, drawing attention to all that was not accomplished in your absence. One way I found to avoid Lynn's wrath was to ensure not only order, but a *new* order.

One afternoon, on the verge of becoming ill, Laurel's stomach began flashing the warning signs of Lynn's eminent return. Attempting to ease her worry, I took the mega phone down from its proper place on the wall and used it to command Laurel's presence in the tack room. Mimicking Lynn, I instructed Laurel to remove the bridles from the wall. She stared at me, hands on her hips, not finding me funny. With alarm, she watched as I pulled bridle after bridle down and *threw* them on the floor, never giving up the impersonation or the mega phone. Exploding with laughter, she followed my lead, grabbed the mega phone and began commanding me to hang the bridles "there, there, no, not here, there."

We laughed ourselves silly and within an hour, had a freshly organized and spotless tack room. Sitting on a tack trunk in the immaculate tack room, we sipped a cold pop, recounted our mischievous diversion and admired our work. We did not immediately tell Lynn the details of how the tack room came to look so splendid, but the efforts were not wasted on her. Tickled with our enterprising efforts, Lynn rewarded us with not only high spirits, but high praise. The incident was one of many Laurel and I shared during our months together at Royal Palm Ranch.

Lynn showed us how to teach the horses tricks and we in kind taught them some tricks of our own. Lynn taught us how to work together as a team, bettered our training methods and, by example, showed us how to run a successful business. She allowed us to have fun, even if at her expense, while building a support system to bolster her success. A fearless leader, Lynn never stopped teaching us, even though some lessons were unintentional.

One morning after a staff meeting, a routine Lynn religiously followed and Laurel reliably agonized over, Laurel scowled at me as she left to saddle Elvis. During the meeting I hastily responded to Lynn's questions about Elvis's progress with particular maneuvers. I bragged about Laurel's skillful training and how well Elvis was responding even though I knew we had never specifically performed the tasks Lynn was inquiring about.

"Why did you say he could do that?" Laurel snarled at me, dreading the ride ahead. "Trust me," I returned, telling her not to worry. We had done our jobs, were good at our jobs and I knew Laurel could make Elvis perform without fail. Confident in our combined abilities, I knew with certainty that Elvis would do exactly as Lynn requested. Although we had not followed Lynn's methods to the code, I knew what I knew: we were a good team.

The ride tested Laurel's trust in me and the work we did together. The duo performed without a glitch, with Elvis responding to every request by Lynn exactly as directed. Relieved and proud, the bond between friends grew tighter. As we worked side by side, we learned not only to trust each other but just how important having that trust is to a relationship. Lynn had us ride specific horses at home and would switch us at the horse show, putting us on a horse we did not regularly school at home. If any of us were to show successfully, it was imperative we trust our teammate's assessment and follow their directions to the tee.

I remember one horse Lynn showed but hadn't ridden at home in months. Before showing, Laurel warned Lynn not to say anything that rhymed with "whoa" to slow the horse. Lynn notoriously talked to the horses and taught us how to use verbal cues successfully. Laurel and I both were proponents of horses coming to a complete flat stop at the word "whoa" each and *every* time and taught them to do so. Just as Lynn was approaching a long rail in front of the judge, wanting her horse to ease up, she said "slow" and the horse planted all four feet in the ground, stopping dead in his tracks. Lynn took full responsibility for the error and praised Laurel for her skillful training and belief in her horse's ability to obey.

Laurel and I worked our tails off. Not only physically, but personally, we both had to make concessions to make the program work. Laurel and I laughed, defended and protected each other. We grew up professionally and became lifelong friends — champions to the other's success. Laurel was crowned Miss Farm Implement that fall. She stood in the bucket of the front end loader waving to her fans who peered at her from behind stall doors. I sang "Here She Comes" and drove her down the barn aisle. She looked stunning in her Sorel boots and insulated coveralls with curly blond tendrils peeking out from beneath her knit cap. Unfortunately, I was the only one there to witness this grand procession and there were no recording devices to mark her victory in history.

Laurel saw, shoveled, fell down, got stuck and drove in her first snow while living in Michigan — preparing her for her eventual move to Lake Tahoe where she currently resides with her family. Laurel continues to show Quarter Horses along with her daughters. Occasionally our paths cross at a distant horse show. Through the years, she continues to be my number one fan supporting me through miles of terrain, shared competition and forsaken promises. I may have indulged her by letting her curl my hair before a night out on the town but she has more than indulged me by sticking with me, breaking my somber manner and lightening the seriousness of the work place.

Prepared not to like her, she is today one of my most trusted friends. She helped me learn to rely on the character of people, good and bad, and not be disappointed when their character did not respond as I wanted. She trusted my instincts, which in turn deepened my trust in them too. I am not sure if I reciprocated any lessons for Laurel, I can only hope that I did. Our time together at Royal Palm Ranch was the most fun I have ever had working and the hardest I have ever worked to have fun. Even today, with not a hair out of place, the picture perfect wife, mother and showman, she reminds me that friends come in all kinds of packages.

*Sometimes when you think you have it
all figured out, and don't need anyone or anything,
someone comes along to show you
what you didn't know you were missing and
fills a void with an impenetrable epoxy.*

Lynn and Peter with A Wild And Crazy Guy
December 1983 in winter wonderland

After this picture was taken, Lynn offered to get a picture of Laurel and I together with Lynn in the sleigh. A Wild And Crazy Guy, aka, E.T., now tired and angry from pulling the heavy sleigh through the deep snow, flashed warning signs, perhaps a foreboding. Unhappy with the situation, I kept one leg out the side. Laurel told me to lighten up, get my leg back in the sleigh and have a little fun. Seconds later, as we trotted down a hill toward the photographer, the sleigh hit E.T. and tipped over on its side. With one leg already outside the sleigh, I grabbed Laurel and pulled her out with me. The sleigh flipped over, throwing Lynn out the other side. With the heavy sleigh banging against E.T. and E.T. running free, he ran around the corner of the barn, tearing the sleigh into a dozen pieces.

Trust, so often unappreciated until it is lost,
sometimes, can never be regained.

**Lynn on A Wild And Crazy Guy with Stephanie,
owner Mary Byers and Laurel**

What a team. A Wild And Crazy Guy, aka E. T., was Lynn's best horse that year. Mary, a favorite customer and a great lady to work for, always encouraged this crazy team, becoming one of Lynn's longstanding loyal allies. More than comrades, we built a relationship based on trust and became lifelong friends.

Allyson Coe with Rogous Boy
1988 World Champion Amateur Working Hunter
Husband Ed and Stephanie

Rogous Boy, aka Radar, was an outstanding hunter, albeit one leaded. A bit of a rogue, he preferred to land on his left lead and because of soundness issues, changed leads with difficulty, if he changed at all. He was tough, which translated to long hours of preparation, causing more physical pain that added to the problematic lead change.

In order to be considered for a prize, Radar had to land on the correct lead over the last fence in each line. Not an easy feat for the most accomplished rider, Allyson had to be perfect, her ride exact and, naturally, it had to look effortless. She left Oklahoma City, not only World Champion, but first on all five cards. Tears of steel were the precursor to her unflinching nerve and focus.

Chapter 15

Steel

My mother and sister, Jennifer, moved to Argyle, Texas in 1984. Originally a stop along the Texas and Pacific Railway en route to Fort Worth it became a community of gentlemen ranchers in the late twentieth century. Just 20 miles from the newly built Dallas Fort Worth airport, Argyle was home to many pilots as well as commuters to the DF W metroplex.

Argyle sits just below the apex of the Golden Triangle of Denton, Dallas and Fort Worth. Dotted with small farms and ranches, populated predominately by Hunter/Jumpers, the land offered fertile ground for the horse business.

Soon after Mom moved south, I left Bessemer, Michigan and moved to Argyle. Fulfilling a promise to myself, I enrolled in the University of North Texas in Denton, fifteen minutes from Argyle. So angered at my decision to quit school and work for Lynn, my father hoped to dissuade me by withdrawing all financial support – present and future. Far from deserting me, he took me to a Friday night fish fry whenever our schedules permitted during my time at Lynn's. Now, still in Wisconsin and thrilled that I enrolled in school, he offered to help pay for tuition. But I was my father's daughter. Too headstrong and proud to accept his generosity, I hung my shingle outside my mother, Sally's, big barn. Hoping to goad me in another direction, my father instead strengthened my resolve. Fearless and fresh from the employ of the renowned Lynn Salvatori

Palm, I jumped headlong into training horses in the heart of horse country and Texas became home to my new training business.

Most of the North Texas Quarter Horse trainers settled north of Denton in Aubry and Pilot Point. The majority trained western and halter horses. Operating south of Denton helped make my business unique in a couple of ways. Closer to the DFW commuting riders' homes, I rode a traditional stock horse breed in the "English" discipline and I gave lessons. Plus, I had just studied under the reigning Hunt Seat "Queen."

As horses started to trickle in, a small following developed. One horse led to another and soon a real business sprouted. At the beginning, clients came from close to home. That was the case with Allyson. She and her husband, Ed, lived a few miles down the road from us. Allyson had a big handsome gray gelding she showed over fences and in flat or rail classes. The Coes worked out of a tidy little barn on their ranch where Ed could rope and Allyson could school her hunter while keeping an eye on her newborn daughter.

In 1985, Allyson qualified her gelding, Paul, for the AQHA World Championship Show in Oklahoma City. The AQHA World Championship Show requires an invitation to show. Points earned between July 31 of the previous year and August 1st of the current year count towards qualification. All but the previous year's winners have to qualify during that period in order to compete at the two week event.

Of the 3,000,000 horses registered with the American Quarter Horse Association, less than half of one percent qualify for one of the AQHA World Championship Shows. Of the roughly 6,000 who qualify, less than half of those actually show at one of the World Shows. Each year AQHA crowns approximately 60 World Champions and fewer than twenty percent of the participants actually earn a prize while competing there. It is truly an elite group that earns the right to show at one of

AQHA's World Championship Shows — a right reserved for the very dedicated few, willing to withstand the hardships it takes to qualify and compete.

For many, just qualifying fulfills a lifetime goal. Having the invitation to hang on their walls alongside other win pictures is a satisfying achievement worth bragging about. Competing at this prestigious event is intimidating to the point that many who qualify can never overcome their nerves enough to actually enter and compete. For those who compete, it is the biggest stage upon which they play — the trophy the most coveted.

Allyson qualified Paul in both the Amateur and Open Hunter Hack. Showing (and winning) in the open events against the professionals took some moxie; an indication of Allyson's readiness to compete at a high level. That she did so without the help of a horse trainer made it all the more impressive.

But that was Ally: tall and beautiful, confident and commanding, she epitomized the successful woman. Husband, career, daughter, great rider; she had it all. Looking for a coach to help prepare for the event, she came to me. Flattered she asked for my help, excited to have my first client to take to the prestigious show in Oklahoma City, we practiced with a goal in mind.

Preparation once there went well. Allyson and Paul schooled like pros. Settling into their horse show routine, they appeared to be performing like clockwork. Ally seemed confident, poised and on top of her game. Her confidence bolstered mine making me feel like I belonged at this important event.

All entries in riding classes at the AQHA World Championship Show must first compete in a preliminary performance earning the right to show in their respective finals performance. Five judges place the class according to their individual preference. After throwing out each entry's high and low placing, scores of the remaining three judges are averaged.

The fifteen highest ranking entries are brought back for the finals performance held on a later date during the show.

In Allyson's event, each horse went into the show arena individually and performed. After jumping two jumps, the top twenty horses were called back for rail work. From the top twenty, five were eliminated and the remaining fifteen came back later to ride for the trophy.

Before entering the arena for their performance, horses and riders are loaded into a chute or alley in front of the entry gate. Coaches are allowed to accompany riders down the chute to a certain point. Two or three horses prior to entering the show arena, everyone must leave as the rider awaits his or her turn to show. Preventing any attempt to influence the judges through a close association with a trainer, the rider must enter the arena gates alone and unassisted.

In the warm up pen outside the chute, Paul had been fly sprayed, hooves polished and his muzzle oiled. Ally's husband gave his "good luck" wishes and left us before Ally entered the chute. Standing with Allyson, rag in hand, we went over the details of her job in the show pen as we inched closer to the entrance. Dusting off her boots, I looked up intending to say something smart. Suddenly, to my shock and horror, she burst into tears! Holy crap — what was happening?

"What's wrong?" I asked. "What's the matter?"

Nothing like this had ever happened before. I had no idea what was going on — should I console, cajole or scold? Where was my confident and capable student? What happened to the poised, commanding, always in control Allyson I knew? All of a sudden, I felt terribly under equipped!

This was my first time as a World Show coach — and I needed a coach! Like every college freshman, I liked and took psychology, but I had no formal training for a meltdown at the gate. The gateman was calling my name, demanding I leave the alley. Allyson had to move ahead and I had to go. I backed away, seriously confused and conflicted.

At a loss for words, but knowing I had to say something I yelled, "You're fine, you'll do great — you look great."

What lame advice. Feelings of helplessness had not been part of the repertoire in my prior training and coaching. Left with nothing else to do, I ran into the stands to see her go. The horse before Allyson's was leaving and the entry gate was opening for Allyson. With bated breath, I nervously waited for the unknown.

A pretty head on a meticulously braided mane led the team through the gate. With ears pricked forward, the handsome gray gelding caught your attention. Allyson, elegantly turned out, rode in tall. Together they created a beautiful picture trotting into the arena. Allyson picked up the canter at the cone and established an authoritative hand gallop.

She held her head up as she confidently rounded the corner galloping toward the two fences that stood in a line. Leaving the corner, her demeanor dwindled. Shrinking, Allyson approached as if wading into a pool of icy water. Paul responded like air coming out of a balloon, slowing his pace as the fence neared. Then, just before the fence, Paul added a short little extra step and hopped over the fence.

With slumped shoulders, I left the arena to meet Allyson as she exited the show arena. Her eyes were wet again. Disappointed in herself, this time the tears were from anger. Allyson knew she had not done her part to put in a stellar performance. Lacking certainty, she stopped riding which allowed Paul to make the decisions. He lazily took the easy way out chipping in to the first fence and ruining any chance of making the call back.

Open week still ahead, Allyson had another class with a chance to redeem herself. Unfortunately, it was the tougher of the two she had entered. She would compete with better riders on the best horses in the open division. AQHA open classes are open to all levels of riders. They are the only class where professionals can show another individual's horse. Hired guns from each discipline's top tier of professionals were flown in to show in any one of the many open events held during open week at the World Show. They would be among the seasoned professionals Allyson would show against in the Senior Hunter Hack. Allyson would likely be the only amateur/owner showing against the pros in her class.

Once again, Allyson and Paul schooled well. For a second time they went through their midnight practice with flawless rides. We braided, groomed, polished and prepared to show another time. Once again, Ed patted Ally on the knee, wished her good luck and left us on our way to the chute. And once again, Allyson burst into tears as her turn approached.

Surprised, but this time not shocked, I came back with a strong tone. I knew nothing was wrong — just a case of jitters. I spoke firmly, instructing her to keep her eyes up over the second fence and to maintain her pace until she landed on the other side of the second fence. Taking a harsh tone, I mustered one last retort:

"KEEP YOUR EYES UP!" I yelled.

Sitting on your horse in the chute going into the World Show arena a million thoughts run through your head. Everything you hoped, dreamed and spent years working for will be over in a matter of minutes, sometimes seconds. Win or lose, expectations, angst, fear, elation and disappointment clash, compounded by the pressure of the desire to win. The result of years of preparation concluded in a few short seconds. The outcome determines your future goals, dreams — even your livelihood — if you are a professional. Leaving Allyson with all these thoughts running through her head, I hoped she could concentrate on that one thing.

Once again, I ran into the stands to watch my team perform. This time Ally kept her eyes up and maintained pace and authority through the line. She had a good trip, met her fences — and her goal. The rest was up to the judges. The judges liked what they saw and Allyson and Paul made the finals in the open division! Cause for celebration.

Becoming a finalist at the AQHA World Championship Show put you in a different league as a competitor. As a rider, you were now part of an elite group and the envy of your rivals. Fans, judges, peers and challengers from all over the country would see you compete as a member of this exclusive club. For Allyson, an amateur riding as a finalist with the professionals, it was especially significant. Buoyed by becoming a finalist at her first World Show, Allyson schooled with more confidence, secure in her preparation for the final's performance. She was back — brilliant as ever, pumped and ready for the finals.

Finals weekend at the AQHA World Championship Show is a big event in the Quarter Horse world. People fly in from all over the world to compete or watch their horses, friends, family and great riders vie for title of World Champion. Friends and stable mates affectionately wished Ally well as they hurried to settle into a seat and watch the finals.

Allyson drew up eighth in the draw. As we once more crept down the chute, I ran the grooming rag over them, rattling off instruction. "Establish your pace early," I told her as I wiped her boots and greased Paul's muzzle. "And ***maintain it*** until you gallop to your stop."

Show preparation progressed as planned. Relieved, I could leave with the assurance they were ready to show. Looking up to make sure Allyson was listening, she squinted toward the pen and nodded her head. Almost on cue, it happened *again* — she burst into tears. "Take a breath," I murmured to myself as much as to Allyson.

No longer surprised, I just barked at her. "Keep your eyes up and PRESS TO THE JUMP," I hollered harshly as the steward again called for my departure from the chute.

This time, her ride stayed strong; determined, Allyson rode Paul to the perfect distance where he jumped with grace and courage. Allyson, rewarded with a ninth place ribbon in her class, was ecstatic. Coming in an unknown, her first time at the AQHA World Show, showing in the *open* division, the results were outstanding. We were all extremely proud. Allyson had now joined the ranks of Top Ten finishers at the AQHA World Championship Show.

In the years that followed, Allyson and I would make more trips to the World Show. Allyson was my first student to win a World Championship. She qualified and showed in four more classes during the years I was privileged to work with her, taking home a total of three World Championship titles.

And each time, just before leaving her in the chute, she would expel a quick tear. After which — eye on the prize — she would lay out a flawless performance. Tears were like alloy; the steel Allyson used when she rode through the gates in Oklahoma City. That steel enabled her to concentrate on the *one* thing she had to do once she entered the arena.

> *An unflinching character can be developed.*
> *As alloys are melted to make steel*
> *So too are imperfections fused to build strength.*

Photo Courtesy Harold Campton

Allyson Coe on Wee Pete at the 1990 AQHA World Show Amateur Working Hunter.

Just moments after a tearful preparation at the back gate, Allyson's ability to turn her emotion around and stay focused is evident in her gaze. She was rewarded with another World Championship title.

Turning the tears off like a light bulb, Allyson exchanged one habit for another. Changing her attitude, she turned misses into hits, losses into wins.

Photo Courtesy Don Trout

**Jill Martin on Matt with Stephanie,
Wally Martin and Karma**

Winning another buckle for
All-Around Novice Amateur on
her quest to win a saddle.

Chapter 16

Teachers

Giving lessons were the main source of income during my first years in Texas and continued to generate new clients. Very few successful North Texas Quarter Horse trainers were willing to give lessons. Established in their niche, they did not need or like to give lessons. I did.

Many long term clients started with lessons. They would bring their horse to my ranch to get instruction once a week, once a month or once in a while. Word of mouth, always the best advertisement, soon brought a nice group of thirsty students.

The first session with a new client is always interesting. You never know how scary a horse might be and whether it will become a liability — to you, your place or even themselves. Riders' descriptions of their ability are notoriously either overstated or understated. Predicting their level of competency or their receptiveness to instruction is impossible to do over the telephone.

On a warm Texas evening with the sun still high in the sky, I waited for a new client to arrive after work for her first lesson. When the Martins pulled in, I heard them before I saw them. A barking Rottweiler bared her teeth from inside the noisy blue Ford van. Kicking up gravel, they towed a rusty old two horse bumper pull trailer, its tongue hanging close to the ground.

Jill jumped out appearing tiny, even timid, next to her husband, Wally. Anything but small, his words were accented by a distinct East Texas drawl. Taking turns, they described the nervous black mare that flew backwards out of the trailer creating enough of a ruckus to bring Ezequiel, my barn manager, running out from his evening chores. As I listened, the mare pawed her way through Ezequiel's meticulously manicured grass. Spinning from side to side, the flaky mare, Dawn, tossed her head and screamed at the top of her lungs. This could prove to be an interesting night.

With shaky hands but a firm voice, Jill saddled up. While she warmed up, Wally continued to give background information. He proudly told of Dawn's historic place in their family and her upbringing at their East Texas homestead. Jill's description of her riding ability had been pretty accurate. Typical of the good people they were, Jill was a better rider than she described. Her horse, however, looked to present more obstacles than the Martins would likely want to hear. Telling people their homebred darling may not cut muster is never an easy task.

After the lesson, I contemplated my new clients as I watched them pull out of the driveway. It did not look like their rig could make it to one more lesson, much less withstand the rigors of going up and down the road to horse shows. I also wondered how they would afford more lessons, or, heaven forbid, a new horse. Showing horses is not a cheap hobby at *any* level and, from all outward appearances, the Martins could not afford it.

For the better part of a year, Jill took lessons diligently taking the instruction and working to improve her skills and prepare Dawn for shows. Eventually, the pair was ready to go to the horse show. Dawn's spookiness made preparation a bit tricky. A worrier, she did not have much trust in people, disliked other horses and insisted on whirling around to face her opponents – the other horses! Fractious under the best of circumstances, her ability to handle commotion was about to be put to the test in the chaotic climate of the horse show.

Jill introduced Dawn to every nook and cranny of the arena, letting her look at every ominous shadow, doorway, break in the wall or sign of advertisement hung around the arena. When Jill finally got into the show ring the mare became so frenzied Jill had to dismount while the competition concluded. Although not the outcome we hoped for, it unfortunately confirmed my initial opinion.

Disappointment comes easy at horse shows. There was no need to make the Martins suffer more than their fair share. The horse presented a challenge I did not think could be trained out of her. It was time to have a serious talk about Jill's future in the show ring. We had already invested another show season on this horse and more time would not change her personality. Somehow, I had to tell them that the beautiful black mare they had lovingly pulled from her mother's belly back home in Dangerfield, did not have what it took to be a winner for Miss Jill. Wally's presence filled most rooms and the office in my barn was not very big. The combination of Texas heat and the upcoming discussion made the air feel especially sticky. Much to my relief, the meeting went well. Entirely aware of the mare's limitations, the Martins accepted my guidance with grace and imminent resolve.

The easy part over, dollars were the next topic to be broached. It is not unusual for the top tier of enthusiasts to pay more for their horse than the average person pays for their house. Working for working people, I had a firm handle on how much it would take to buy Jill the horse she needed. Jill and Wally surprised me. After five months working together it should have come as no surprise that the Martins could easily afford the budget I proposed. They were as unpretentious as people could be; driving a crummy old van they could have been millionaires the way they lived. Sensible, but certainly more than I anticipated, their budget was ample and soon we were looking at horses.

Matt was found close to home. A young horse that had been on some trainer's back burner, he was a cute little bay gelding, good mover and showed lots of potential. Matt fit the bill for Jill. It did not take long before Jill and her new steed were winning everywhere. My customers nicknamed Jill the "Buckle Queen". Never again to be confused with timid, Jill was dogged in her quest to win a new show saddle. Considered the grand daddy of all prizes, Jill won many buckles along the road to claim her new saddle.

The Martin's had horses with me for more than twenty years. They traveled with my show string all over the country — even long after I left Texas. From Arizona to Ohio, Tulsa, Duluth and all parts in between, Jill and Wally were there every step. Win or lose, they always had a smile, a kind word and a generous assist.

Watching their rusted out trailer pull away from my ranch after their first lesson in Argyle, I could never have guessed that three decades later they would continue to be my number one fan. The old blue van never slowed us down and Wally was always there to fix *my* flat tire, patch *my* radiator hose or get *my* alternator repaired.

All those years I thought I was teaching Jill and students like her. But in truth, they were teaching me. Their continued support has shored up my confidence when it was low; their humble aid rescued my stubborn temperament more than once. The kindness and generosity shown through the years overwhelms me with gratitude. Their enthusiastic devotion has championed *my successes* beyond my biggest dreams for them.

Thirty years after the Martins pulled away from my Argyle ranch, the following quote by William Arthur Ward printed from my fax machine, sent by Jill:

The mediocre teacher tells. The good teacher explains. The superior teacher demonstrates. The great teacher inspires.

There could be no greater compliment.

From left: Jilll Martin, Julianne Hornig, Lauri Smith (Rice), Sarah Smith, Stephanie, Wally Martin, Jason Hagberg (assistant trainer), Katie and Mary Bowman

My teachers.
Helping celebrate my birthday in 2000 at a
horse show in Windom Minnesota.

Photo Courtesy Pennau Photography

Stephanie on Fred stepping over a log in perfect stride

If you want different results
change your approach.
A new attitude will
bring about a new ending.

Chapter 17

Change Your Approach

Horse shows often have some type of class where the individual is asked to perform a pattern or go over obstacles. It is part of their test and rewards excellence, proficiency and athleticism in the horses.

Western and stock horse classes often use poles to walk, jog or lope over. Riders are asked to perform specific gaits and maneuver around or at cones to test their horsemanship skills. Faux fences are set in an arena to test a hunter's ability to jump to great heights. Dressage riders use letters on the side of the arenas as reference to execute certain maneuvers. Every discipline within each breed has its own description or definition of a test. But one thing is certain across breeds; a horse's ability to meet obstacles in stride determines the winners.

Practice for riders, especially those who compete, often involves the use of poles, cones, letters, jumps or a combination of obstacles. They are used to mark specific points at which riders are to perform particular maneuvers, to outline the detail of a pattern to be performed or as boundaries to contain a particular course to be ridden.

One day while riding in from the pasture, I saw a student struggling in the arena. She was trying to lope over logs that were laid out in the arena. The student, Susan, had been riding with me earlier in the week, watching while I schooled a horse over the same logs she now rode over. Susan attempted to duplicate a favorite technique I use to teach horses and riders to meet obstacles in stride.

Two poles are simply dropped on the ground in a parallel line with enough distance between the poles to lope over, at least twelve feet. The poles are not measured to any predetermined distance. Rather they are randomly placed making the duo adjust the horse's stride in order to meet the next pole. This makes the team determine the best way to get through the poles. An especially "scopey" horse will make the appropriate adjustment. More often than not, the horse needs a little assistance from the rider, particularly in the beginning.

A horse's stride at the canter can vary in length from a six foot slow lope to a full 12-foot or more gallop to cover the ground. Sometimes the ground covering stride is to get to the next fence and sometimes to outrun a cow. An outsider might think that the horse's height would be the main factor in determining stride length. But the rider has the ability to control the horse's stride length through the use of their hands and legs collecting and extending the horse's step.

Whether approaching a jump, a lead change or a stop, the horse's legs have to be in the right place in order to perform the maneuver with precision. This imaginary "box" is the ultimate spot for the horse to leave the ground. Trying to find this box, Susan picked up her canter, established her pace and began going over the logs. Each time, as she tried to put her horse, Mack, in the box, she invariably picked up the same pace, rounded the corner from the same place and approached the obstacle the same way.

Most of the time, Susan and Mack missed the appropriate distance. Mack broke gait, hit the log, leapt from a huge distance, hopped like a rabbit or split the log with his legs (this has the most potential for danger over a jump). Mack continued to flounder as his footfall missed the box. Frustrated, Susan kept loping over the logs. Invariably, she repeated the exercise in the same way again and again with the same results. Her outcome never changing, aggravation settled in. Failing to see any alternatives, Susan disciplined Mack even though *she* controlled the timing, position and direction of the horse. Her results, consequently, worsened. Seeing this on my way in from the pasture, I asked Susan to take a break while I put my horse up.

Out in the arena, we began to experiment with different approaches. Overcome with frustration, Susan had been concentrating so hard on changing the *results* she could not see the options before her.

In fact, Susan had several options. She could make the horse go faster (lengthening the stride) or make the horse go slower (shortening the stride). She could cut the corner (shortening the distance to cover in front of the obstacle) or go deeper into the corner (putting more distance in front of the obstacle).

Testing the options, Susan found that she was most comfortable with changing her approach to the corner. By shortening the corner, she had less time to worry and change her mind, which could change her horse's stride length (a result of which she was unaware). Now, she realized, she had several options. Once she discovered her choices, she understood there were not only many alternative approaches, but infinitely more outcomes. That she could affect all of them was a revelation.

By going faster, slower or changing the angle of her approach, Susan boosted her ability to get in the box. Through practice, her success rate improved as she learned to try different techniques, changing her approach to make an adjustment. She learned to meet the logs in stride while staying within her comfort zone.

Finding the most comfortable approach comes only after trying different methods. It takes time as well as a fresh outlook to break old habits. But change *can* happen. Logs, like obstacles in life, present opportunities to change the outcome.

Hitting *your* stride may only be a step away!

Photo Courtesy of Katie Bowman

Stephanie approaching a problem from a different angle

Change, though not easy for everyone,
is possible.
Only when we are truly
able to change our attitude or approach,
will a visible difference be made clear.

Mickey Dator with Stephanie in the saddle
Owner Lee Hensen holding medallion

Deciding when to quit and when to do something one more time, may be an art form. But if someone else can see the results coming, you ought to be able to discover how to feel its impending arrival for yourself.

Chapter 18

One More Time

How many times had I told myself "one more time" only to try twenty eight more times, unable to find a place to stop? Such was the case with the log in the western riding for me and Mickey Dator. Mickey Dator was a cute little red roan gelding and my first horse to qualify in the Western Riding for the AQHA World Championship Show. His big brown eyes popped alongside the broad forehead with a little star and a constant look of alarm. His sole job in life was to tote his owner around in the western pleasure class, a pleasant event where the horse travels around the arena showing off their slow easy gaits.

Western pleasure is a class that evaluates the horse's ability to provide a comfortable smooth ride; the horse should appear to be a "pleasure" to ride. It may have originated as a class to show off a colt's potential to be useful for more difficult jobs, like reining, western riding, trail or working ranch horse classes. Today, it has morphed into a highly competitive, specialized, event. Although the class is one of the most popular at the horse show, it did not appeal to me. Schooling for the event seemed tiresome, uninteresting and the repetition of the remedial exercises boring.

Horses get bored with the event, too. Drilling the seemingly monotonous exercises can eventually make many of them dull and resentful. Teaching the horse how to do other things keeps them fresh. Mickey was happy to go along doing what his rider asked him to do and took good care of his owner, Lee. Tedious schooling for pleasure inevitably led me to teach Mickey more challenging techniques. He presented little resistance with his training, going over logs, maneuvering around cones, side passing and eventually learning to change leads with ease. Before long we were competing in the western riding and trail class.

The western riding class has a single log that horses must traverse at the jog and the lope. Mickey learned to western ride at a time when AQHA offered only one pattern for the class. It started with a gait which the rider opened, passed through and closed. The horse then picked up the jog, jogged over the log, and started the lope at the far end of the arena. The horse loped back down the arena weaving through cones, then criss-crossed back up the arena, changing leads before each change of direction, a total of eight times. The rider negotiated the lope log as they made their third turn around a cone.

The dreaded log has been the demise of many great western riding trips. It often takes a team's score down measurably from first to last or not placing at all. Like so many problems, the real difficulty often comes from the rider, not the horse. Horses adjust their stride to step over objects on the ground all day long without the assistance of a rider. Left to their own, they would never intentionally step on a log lying in their path. By the time horses are accomplished enough to have qualified for the AQHA World Championship Show, they have been over plenty of logs with a rider and shouldn't spook from a plain old wooden pole sitting on the ground. But that does not mean they won't leap it, take a stutter step, hit it, roll it or break gait over it causing one's score to reflect the setback.

Mickey's wary nature compelled him to be extraordinarily cautious. He wanted no part of touching any scary log, no matter how innocently it sat on the ground. At first afraid of it, he veered over it or jumped it like a deer clearing the four inch log by two feet high. Had he seen it in the pasture, he would have stepped over it as naturally as he would have eaten the alfalfa. But in the show pen, the log took on a different dimension.

The dilemma for me lay in the angle of the approach. The log in the western riding pattern had to be traversed while rounding a corner. If the approach was not perfect, the horse not bent in the perfect arc, it appeared to the horse that he could skip the log and go around it. On our path to qualify for the World Show I tried every angle and combination I could come up with. We batted a 50/50 average of hits and misses. When we missed, Mickey took a giant leap across the log, his faith tried, as he hoped the log would not attack or move. The results had been good enough to get qualified, but the odds left me out of play at a competition like the World Championship Show.

At horse shows, practice arenas provide fertile ground for education. The warm up pen can easily be considered a class room for horsemen. Sharing the arena with other professionals, proficient in their field, opportunities for learning were plentiful. Teasing each other after biffs, misses and near disasters, the practice pen staged comic relief as well. Just hanging out, arms perched on the rail or sitting on the fence watching others school, you learned a ton. A sponge, I thrived in this pool of my contemporaries.

Jackie Krshka, a three time World Champion in western riding, lived north of Argyle outside Oklahoma City. Traveling to the same shows, her students competed against mine in many events and we shared much time over the fence at the back gate. As fellow competitors, we also practiced together in the warm up pen. Jackie generously offered tips. Accepting my questions as the flattery they were, she took interest in my cute little gelding encouraging our participation. She reminded me over and again that confidence comes from repetition, from keen preparation with successful rehearsals. Advancing my knowledge and increasing my determination, I left horse shows with more than just prizes. Taking her words literally, I went home and practiced repeatedly, over and over again, searching for perfection I knew would never come.

Each November Oklahoma City hosts the AQHA World Championship Show. Mickey's trip to the prestigious event marked my first time to compete in the western riding at the World Show. To this day, the western riding class is one of the most impressive classes to watch. Prominent trainers earn great respect and are celebrated for their ability to train horses for this event. I had been one of those people sitting in the stands, Diet Coke in hand, watching every move made by the esteemed trainers as they competed in this distinguished class. Fascinated by their ability, there were years I spent dreaming of showing alongside them, earning their respect as a fellow horseman, still trying to prove I was a hand.

Now that day was here. My desire to have a good go, mistake free, one without biffs, ticks or misses, far outweighed my thoughts of winning a *big prize*. Big wins in Oklahoma City were years in the making and I hoped this debut trip would lay the groundwork for a chance at such a win. The purpose of this trip, my only real goal, was to put in a respectable ride – to not embarrass myself, but to be one of them, to earn their respect. The pressure is intense when competing at the World Show. The ride, over in minutes, often took several years of training and competing to achieve. The tiniest of mistakes leaves horses out of the running for any chance of a prize. Simply putting in a good ride had to be my only goal — that meant getting over the log without a leap.

Tension runs deep during preliminaries in Oklahoma City. With jagged nerves, I entered the small warm up arena next to the show pen to prepare Mickey for our preliminary competition. The legendary trainers rode aggressively vying for a position to practice the single log laid out for all exhibitors to practice over. Intimidated by their uncompromising stature and insistent line of travel, they easily pushed Mickey and me out of their way riding as if they owned the log, circling it time and again. I hovered on the edges of the arena abjectly looking for a line to ride on. When finally we entered the arena to show, it was a relief to be out of the crowd and it felt good to be in the pen by ourselves. We advanced successfully through the preliminaries to the finals held later in the week — a big leap in the right direction for me.

Thrilled but equally nervous with the stands full of onlookers, judges and peers, Mickey and I prepared for the finals competition. Having ridden earlier in the day in a beautiful field on the far side of the fairgrounds, Mickey felt good, ready to show. We had our quiet time to school, our time for contemplation; now we were ready for the heat. Jogging in, I eased into the group of the fourteen other finalists, the elite. This time, I attempted to ride more aggressively. Trying to fit in, I rode to a place in line for the log, vying for *my turn* to lope over the log one more time.

By the time finals come around, many of the washed out teams had gone home making more room for the finalists to prepare for their final's performance. Jackie, confident in her finalist horse, kept one eye on Mickey and me. I loped over the log again and again each time telling myself, "one more time." Knowing I needed to quit but still unsatisfied with my imperfections, I kept going, unable to stop. In my mind, I repeated "one more time" and headed for the log one more time. Mickey, a willing student repeated the exercise. While I reached for some elusive perfection, Mickey's enthusiasm waned. With visions of western pleasure clouding his mind and the twenty-eighth time looming closer, boredom took a firm hold of Mickey's mind and his tired legs.

Jackie, not only a World Champion herself, had also coached many students to World Championships. She witnessed plenty of students leave their best performance in the practice pen. Watching me, she loped a circle around me and said, "Don't have your best ride out here," and kept loping past me. While practice makes perfect, Jackie knew I was on the brink of over schooling. Mickey, quickly reaching the point of frustration, fatigue setting in, tired of the log, and began to drag his toes over the log. My time in the hunter pen had taught me it is often best to quit just after the horse clunked a jump (theoretically, the experience of hitting the jump is a reminder to pick their feet up in the show pen). Flashing back, images of repetitive boring practice and the ensuing apathy, Jackie's words prompted me to stop. I walked over to my assistant for a final dusting off and shot of fly spray while I waited for my turn to show.

Mickey performed like a star, without biffs, ticks, or misses. As I rode out of line to pick up my third place ribbon, I passed the fourth place rider sitting on the previous year's winner. The look on his face was classic — the white ribbon a reminder of the bitter pill he swallowed. On the other hand, I was beaming. Third place, the yellow medallion, proudly placed me amongst the elite in the western riding pen. Congratulations were shared by most of the exhibitors, none spoken more proudly to me than Jackie's acknowledgment of our accomplishment.

Countless times just before entering the arena, while coaching a student or before I push for a little bit more, the words on the tip of my tongue — come back — one more time. It is a constant struggle to know when enough is enough. The battle's outcome unknown until the bitter end, becomes easier to predict with practice. Confidence comes from knowledge; worry from lack of experience. The difference lies in knowing when to quit and when to go for it — one more time.

Nancy (Perlich) Kenway on Royalty in Town
Stephanie coaching from the fence at an Arizona show

As my student, Nancy depended on me to determine when to ask for more, try again or when to stop. As a showman, she had to decide when to press her horse for more and when she had tapped the limits of her horse's capabilities. Now, as a mother, daughter, wife and entrepreneur, she must decide on her own accord, when to try one more time, ask another way or call it a day.

Jennifer Lynn-Eckstrom and Three Eighty aka Jessie

Jennifer became my guinea pig, showing the horses we owned in the amateur events. This gave our horses credibility with someone other than a trainer and helped to make the horses more salable. It worked. Jennifer did not get a second chance to show Jessie. With a favorable first outing, Jessie was sold during the first show we took him to, confirming my feelings that he was a winner.

Chapter 19

Gut Feelings

My mother often jokes that she has no regrets about anything she bought — only the things she didn't buy. Pondering each purchase, shopping with her can be grueling. Unlike her, I am a buyer, not to be confused with a shopper — I buy. I either like it or don't, need it or don't, want it or don't, have to have it or don't want any part of it. Rarely does the decision to buy take much time.

When it came to buying horses, tracking down horses to look at took the most time. Many horses have come into my barn on a whim, the decision to buy taking only a few seconds, often on first glance I knew the horse would somehow come home with me. In the hundreds of horses purchased as prospects or for clients, only a few have I later regretted. All of them shared a common characteristic; they rendered a queer feeling in the pit of my stomach.

Oscar first hit my radar after I received a telephone call from the agent trying to sell him. Billed as a pretty gelding, supposedly he was good minded and easy to get along with; a good mover and talented enough to jump 3' but not 3'6" (a huge discrepancy in the Hunter/Jumper world but acceptable for my needs).

As I pulled into to the hunter barn where the horse was stabled, I was immediately struck by the grandiose entrance. An ornate gate combined wrought iron, stone and copper in a most unusual way. With no horses in sight, the manicured lawn and perfectly placed flower pots seemed better suited for a country club than a barn. Lavishly laid out, it eerily lacked any sense of life. No paddocks with parading horses, no horses nipping at each other over open French doors, no one riding in an arena, no tractors, dogs, kids or kittens were in evidence. It had the feel of an abandoned property.

Countless times I have pulled into a place and a particular horse will catch my eye amidst the many that may be in view. Unleashing a sense that this was the one I came to look at, it's uncanny how many times the one that caught my eye, was indeed the horse I came to look at. With a strange sense of hope and dread, a funny feeling grew. Prudence told me to reserve judgment. But decisions always began formulating in my gut long before the horse was fully presented.

Driving through the grand gates to look at Oscar, the same nagging feeling sprang up. Strangely, the feeling did not arise from a horse catching my eye. Instead the feeling came from a lack of the living. Walking in from the 98-degree Texas heat, the cool of the barn welcomed me, but with an *unwelcomed* chill. The barn, as beautiful on the inside as it was on the outside, had huge stalls, high ceilings, automatic water and fly systems and a floor so clean you could eat off it. Conspicuously quiet, too quiet, the only sound came from the fans whirring high above reinforcing the sense that no one lived here.

The sound of the office door opening startled me. The agent who greeted me matched the description of the surroundings and looked like he had just come from lunch at the Country

Club. Smooth and well groomed, distant but well spoken; his cool persona mirrored the show place.

Walking down the wide alley, we eventually ended up at the stall door of the horse I came to see. Peering in through the polished metal bars, I saw an attractive dark horse, shining like freshly waxed bronze. As the agent swung the heavy mahogany door open, goose bumps appeared on my arms, a chill running through me.

Oscar was everything that I hoped he would be; a rich seal brown, he had a baby doll head, big withers with a deep heart girth capable of carrying a saddle and standing up to hours of riding. Standing in the oversized stall in a bed of fluffy white shavings, he looked expensive.

When the agent went into the stall to put on a halter and lead the horse out, he backed his ears. No big deal, but worth noting — especially since he kept his ears back, head down low, as the agent led him to the grooming area. With a dull expression, the horse tolerated the grooming, uninterested in either of the mere mortals giving him attention. While tacking the horse up, the agent began dropping names of trainers next on his call list. An instant turnoff, the words were a warning to boot. I did not trust this individual but proceeded anyhow.

Then the agent hopped on the horse and cantered away. I was smitten — the horse was a beautiful mover. There were no lies there. I loved the dappled brown gelding's way of going and was immediately captivated by his looks and movement. He looked exactly like the image of my ideal horse, almost.

Ears went back again when I got on, but I already began making excuses; maybe the horse doesn't get turned out enough; perhaps the shady trainer is abusive in his training; the horse will be happier at my place, and so on. I loved the way he moved — the horse was a beautiful package. After a short negotiation, we agreed on a price. At this point, the horse only had to pass a pre-purchase exam before we sealed the deal.

My veterinarian did the pre-purchase giving the horse a clean bill of health. At the end of the physical exam, he asked if I wanted the horse drug tested. The question caught me off guard. Of the scores of horses this vet had pre-purchased for me, he had *never asked that question.*

The horse had just come off of competition. With knowledge of the competition and the horse's placing, I knew Oscar had been drug tested during the horse show. If this agent was running him on an illegal substance, it would not show up in a normal drug screen. Cagey enough not to get busted, trainers who dope their horses always seem to be one step ahead of the drug testers. Besides, with all of the available designer drugs, my vet and I wouldn't have a clue what to look for. Still, the question itself unnerved me and should have rung the alarm louder than it did.

When the horse came home to Argyle, my sister, Jennifer, and I decided to call him Oscar. After all, he was a bit crabby — remember those ears? Well, bad ears turned to bad attitude. Bad attitude turned into bad behavior in the show ring. As it turned out, he needed those big withers because his back carried many wet saddle pads trying to change his disposition. But even hours of riding did not turn this ill-willed horse into a cooperative student. Oscar was fast becoming a loser in my barn.

The warning signs had been there from the moment I drove into the cold unfriendly stable. The slimy agent, the ears, the lack of personality, the dull expression, the excuses, the question from my veterinarian; and that foreboding feeling in my gut that I chose to ignore. Oscar had been a mistake. Now, forgoing the potential for profit, I just wanted out. Although Oscar continued to be a beautiful animal, he was not working in my program and I could not represent him in good conscience. Time to cut my losses; Oscar had to find a new home.

Shortly after Oscar came home to Argyle, I learned that "Ole Slick," the agent who sold Oscar, had a reputation for drugging his horses. Of course I have tried to steer clear of him and his kind ever since. Unfortunately I do not know what ultimately happened to poor sad Oscar. Jennifer tried unsuccessfully to show him. I knew if she could not get him shown, neither could any other amateur. He eventually left on a horse trader's trailer bound for a destination unknown.

Gun-shy, with fewer dollars in my pocket to spend, I tiptoed back into the field of For Sale ads and found another horse to look at. I spotted Jessie standing in a filthy outdoor stall made of portable panels held together with bailing wire. Chickens scattered when I pulled up and eyed the bedraggled horse I undoubtedly came to see. As if a brush had never stroked his hair, he had thistles in his mud packed mane and tail.

He also appeared to need worming. His hip bones protruded sharply, ribs showed above his bloated belly and his hair coat was long and rough. But his ears perked up with the cackling chickens flapping their wings as they cleared a path for my passing. His big brown eyes showed interest as he watched me approach.

To a certain degree, success in the show ring relies on illusion. A judge critiques the image presented to them at that moment in time. They are not asked to see through blemishes or imagine what the horse would look like when cleaned up or training is complete. Looking through the rough stuff is the job of the horse trainer, the bird dog or scout. That was my job, and a hunch formulated as I neared the dilapidated barn.

The old horse trader that greeted me had holes in the jeans he tucked into manure covered boots. *He* hadn't missed any meals and, though he did not need worming, he could have used a dentist. Dread deepened as he spit then wiped his mouth with the back of his hand before taking mine to shake. My stomach did one of those back flips and I wished I could reach for a hand wipe.

Watching Jessie move, I immediately knew I had to have him. Pathetic in his filthy surroundings, he was a great mover, tall, the right color, pretty headed — and — he spoke to me. Something about this scruffy horse stirred emotions and made my heart skip a beat. Excited, giddy with fantasies of wins to come, I saw him slick haired, fattened up with his mane braided, eyes sparkling and ears alert trotting around the show pen. I just took a bath on Oscar and was broke. But somehow, this horse had to be in my barn. The gruff old horse trader, reading me like a book, drove a hard bargain. I ended up trading four horses to get Jessie in my trailer. The horses I traded were well fed, well bred, well cared for and the two of riding age, were well broke! But that did not matter; I had a feeling about Jessie. He had to be mine. Although it took some finagling to acquire Jessie, it took only a few minutes to decide I had to have him.

There have only been a couple of horses since Oscar that resulted in buyer's remorse. Both times, I knew the horse would not work for the client but weakened my resolve and allowed their wishes to override my instinct. I am still learning, but as a rule, the first impression, the feeling that sits deep in my belly, is the bedrock of my best decisions. Learning to filter out the debris is a continual challenge.

Jessie suffered a setback, breaking a splint bone. He underwent surgery, but in time and with training, Jennifer and Jessie were triumphant in the show ring. Unfortunately for Jennifer, they were so successful that he sold after competing at their first show together. He went on to be the first All-American Quarter Horse Congress winner for his new owners and died happily in their care.

We hold the answers in our hearts.
Separating the significant from the pointless
we must look inside, without fear,
trusting ourselves as no one else.

**Fred and Stephanie as they
exited the AQHA World Show arena in 1995**

"Every good gift and every perfect gift is from above"

James 1:17

Chapter 20

Fred – A Gift Horse

There is nothing quite like ending a long day at the horse show with a hot shower, an old movie and fresh pizza delivered to the room. Those were the circumstances on this particular January evening. Sitting on a Scottsdale, Arizona hotel bed munching on a *Veggie Lovers,* I pondered the circumstances surrounding the telephone call I was expecting.

The previous August, another phone call resulted in a new client. The call and subsequent client seemed to materialize from thin air. Most often, clients were people I met at shows. Looking for help or perhaps a change in venue, they were referred by fellow riders, past or present students in my program. Not famous, people did not flock to my stable from nowhere. Kerith, the young lady who called from Montana, would not disclose her source of referral. She had been given the opportunity of a year to show following her graduation from the University of Montana before moving back to her home state of Colorado. Kerith wanted out of the cold of Montana and into the heart of Quarter Horse country. Based on some cryptic referral, she had come to me for guidance. In need of a new horse, a new trainer and a new address, I had been chosen.

At the time, I thought the mystery surrounding her appearance odd, but not one to look a gift horse in the mouth, I accepted the invitation to assist Kerith in her quest. Horse trainers are a nosy lot, and her visit left me with more questions than answers. I remained curious, but my questions remained unanswered. One week after our initial discussion, Kerith flew in to see her new trainer's barn and discuss her future. An hour after her arrival, she was gone — off to look for an apartment closer to Argyle than Billings, Montana. Following a brief narrative, she left me with contact information, a substantial budget, and a dropped jaw.

After our meeting, I quickly went to work looking for Kerith's new horse. She had given me a budget along with a brief, somewhat sketchy, description of what she wanted. Kerith definitely wanted a gelding; that she made clear. She wanted something that could excel in one event or another. Well that was helpful! The horse had to be tall, preferably a dark "hunter" type; one that could do *some* western event but remained stronger in the hunt seat. The description was obscure at best.

Ideally, when purchasing a horse for a client, the client rides the horse prior to committing. Like a test drive, this increases the likelihood that the pair will get along, not fight like siblings. The ride is especially important when the horse is being purchased for the customer's use. It also allows the customer to share in the responsibility of the decision to buy a particular horse taking some of the weight off the trainer's shoulders. When questioned about the logistics of this procedure, Kerith indicated it would not be necessary for her to ride or see the horse. She simply stated she was aware of my reputation and would like whatever I bought for her.

Perhaps this was the reason I had been given such broad shoulders. The moral obligation that came with the responsibility of purchasing Kerith's horse was tremendous. My job entailed finding Kerith a suitable horse and preparing her and the horse for competition. But my personal duty to be accountable meant ensuring Kerith's dreams came true. Until buyers do the work themselves, they have no idea how much time is spent on the phone, how many miles are driven or life threatening rides on horseback are taken. Nor do they understand the responsibility one assumes when taking the job. Not walking in my shoes, it is difficult to understand the burden that comes with the task of buying a horse for someone else. If the horse disappoints the rider in any way, the trainer is saddled with the bulk of the responsibility for the outcome. It is a responsibility I took very seriously.

Kerith wanted to conclude her journey in Oklahoma City at the AQHA World Championship Show. The implication was huge: she wanted a winner and trusted me to find one. Honored, Kerith's trust felt both weighty and heady. What if she did not win a trophy in the *one year* she had given herself with me? What if the horse I purchased did not fulfill her dreams? What if they did not get along or could not get qualified?

Kerith's trust in my ability to make the right decision weighed heavily on my mind. Reaching for another piece of pizza, I chewed over the unlikely circumstances surrounding my task while I waited for the call to come through the hotel telephone. I just had a feeling; this could be *the one.*

As a group, horse trainer's reputations rank either just above or just below that of used car salesmen's. Depending on your most recent experience with either, you may love them or hate them; trust them or refute them. Having quickly grown old in experience, there were very few trainers whose word I trusted. Bob, the trainer whose call I expected, was among the trusted few. He too, had a reputation — as one of the world's greatest horse trainers. He won everything from western pleasure to western riding, working cow horse and reining. If he so desired, he could train a donkey to jump.

The horse he called to tell me about met all of the basic criteria; tall, too tall for Bob's purposes, dark and he was a he. Reinforcing my impression that this horse might be *the one*, anticipation grew as Bob detailed a description of the gelding. Travel plans made, we spoke again to confirm final arrangements. Bob asked if I wanted to see the video tape he made of the horse. In my mind, seeing the tape could only have one of two results — both bad: I would love the tape and hate the horse, or hate the tape and be mad I had to waste two days going to see him!

Having learned my lesson, I went with my gut and flew to Oregon without watching the video tape. Sitting on the airplane, I again pondered the situation. The whole thing was surreal; a nice girl, a talented rider, appears out of the blue giving me free rein to buy *her* dream horse. Apprehensive, I hoped my hunch would bear fruit. Cautiously optimistic, I was fraught with the enormity of the task, pumped about the prospect's potential, yet wary of taking the plunge.

Arriving late in the day, Bob's wife, Christy, picked me up at the airport. As we drove through the lush green Oregon hills, she pointed out local hot spots including the horse's namesake establishment in town. By the time we got to the farm, it was too late to ride. Bob, away at a horse show, left the task of presenting the horse to his assistant. The assistant would ride him the next morning in the daylight of the indoor arena as the cold February rains prevented our riding outside.

Christy uncovered the horse, allowing me to look at him in the stall. Bob excelled in the working horse arena; cow horses and Reiners were his stock and trade. The black gelding standing in the stall in front of me clearly did not fit in. He was huge in comparison to his stable mates, barely fitting in the low ceilinged stall. Laying my eyes on him fueled my feeling and I fought to control my excitement.

Christy prepared dinner and we visited in front of the television in a room filled with trophies. Championship buckles and win pictures from the world's greatest events lined the bookcases. Enveloped in the enchanting atmosphere, Christy and I chatted about their past champions and the prospects for future winning runs standing in the barn.

Following a restless night, I awoke early and waited for movement in the kitchen. As soon as I heard Christy stirring, I got up, said my good mornings and hurried to the barn. Knowing the assistant would be in the barn early, I left Christy making coffee. After the previous evening's brief inspection, I was itching to see the tall dark gelding move.

Christy met us just as we were leading the horse out of the arena. With her coffee in hand, panic flashed quickly in her eyes. In a look of astonishment she inquired what was wrong wondering if something had happened.

"Nothing" I replied. "The horse will work." I loved him.

"Wow" she said, "that was fast!" Indeed it was.

With a couple of hours to kill before we had to leave for the airport, Christy asked if I wanted to see the tape of the black gelding I had just fallen for. We sat in front of the TV this time sipping fresh squeezed lemonade. While we watched the video, she confessed her concerns over my quick departure from the arena.

A crazy neighbor liked to shoot varmints and Christy worried that the black gelding with white around one eye had done something dumb — like spook and buck me off upon hearing a shot fired! Indeed, he had spooked and grabbed his butt, showing his true nature after the startling gunshot. The move may have unnerved some and certainly did reinforce the myth of the white around the eye being an indication of flakiness.

Her concern drew a chuckle. Whether he was unpredictable because of the white around his eye or just because it was in his character, my decision was made; this was the one.

The video Bob and Christy had been sending to prospective buyers was awful. No wonder I was the only one who came to look at this dapper dude. Inwardly, I triumphed; grateful the tape so poorly portrayed this very cool horse.

With the vetting complete, everyone in the barn was anxious to see Kerith's new steed. No one more than Kerith, who was more than a little nervous about the gelding's impending arrival. Brutally honest, intent on full disclosure, I told Kerith about all of the horse's negatives, including the white around his left eye. Nightmares of a wild-eyed, little red mare with a bald face and blue eyes had kept her awake since hearing the details of her new horse. Kerith awaited the geldings arrival with uncertainty.

Within a few weeks, the horse was delivered to a horse show in Tucson, Arizona. Picking him up at the show was an easy way to get him home without having to ship him commercially from Oregon to Texas. He arrived as promised; tall, dark and handsome with white around one eye, his quirky nature self-evident as he spooked at the stall decorations and later let himself out of his stall.

Tucson was a huge show drawing exhibitors from all over the country. Riding Kerith's new horse around in front of the throngs of contenders was delightful. The big gelding was a beautiful mover, fun to sit on and his striking good looks drew the attention of fellow competitors. Like the cat that swallowed the canary, Kerith and I took turns riding him around the fairgrounds getting to know the new horse. Answering the inevitable inquiries upon seeing us on this pretty gelding, several trainers grunted their displeasure when they discovered where the horse came from. Sickened, they had passed on the horse after seeing the tape. It was a move some regretted after seeing the horse in person.

First thing on Kerith's plate was finding a suitable name for the dashing black gelding. Changing a horse's name is believed to bring bad luck by the superstitious. Black horses are also thought to be unpredictable and white around the eyes assumed to be evidence of flakiness. Superstition be damned, we knew the horse was flaky and unpredictable. Never-the-less, he needed a new name. Besides, we were writing our *own* story, one with origins that, to this day, remain unknown to me.

Registered as The Snooty Fox, the previous owner called him Snooty. Bob and Christy called him by the owner's name, a tradition many of us follow. Kerith had an uncle named Bob, so that was out. Kerith, not a *Snooty* kind of girl, wanted to call him Owen — it sounded, well, un-horse like — too hard to say. Although capricious, the horse was a regular guy — extremely good looking with a quirk or two — Kerith and I decided on Fred. In true Texas tradition, Bob was added at the end.

Tickled with our purchase, we loaded Fred Bob into my Texas bound trailer where his new home awaited. Still cautiously optimistic, I was giddy with anticipation. The opening lines now written, this horse came with high expectations – expectations I intended to fulfill.

All gifts are gifts from above
providing reason to be grateful.
The origins of a gift are unimportant.
Its value will be determined by how well the receiver
applies the benefits, both good and bad.

Ann Marie Kulungowski, MD on her wedding day in 2008
Pediatric Surgery Fellow
at the Children's Hospital in Denver, Colorado

You can take the girl out of horse show
But you can never take the horse show out of the girl.

Chapter 21

Winners

Annie started riding with me when she was thirteen years old. Her mother drove 500 miles from their south Texas Harlingen home for Annie to ride, train and show out of my Argyle training barn. Because of the distance, along with her mother's job as the sole provider, Annie usually stayed several days when she came to ride.

Summers for Annie were spent in Argyle not Harlingen. Special occasions, holidays and birthdays often occurred away from home and family. Instead, they were spent with her extended horse show family in North Texas.

Annie was an excellent student, both at school and at the ranch. She was astute, independent, witty and dedicated. Respectful and ambitious, she was a girl of many talents. At sixteen she was accepted into a program for gifted teens. She finished out her last years of high school at the University of North Texas, just 10 minutes from the ranch.

Getting a two year jump start on her classmates back in Harlingen, she was also able to feed her habit – riding horses! It was her escape when professors were tough, fellow students fickle, Mom too far away or she just plain needed a break.

Having spent so much time at the ranch, it was like a second home to her; she had long ago become part of my family.

Her senior year of high school, sophomore year of University, Annie and her horse *Here Comes Cash*, were smoking in the show ring. With her strict school schedule, she had little time for horse shows. When she went — it had to be to a big show with big numbers. She simply could not afford the time away from her studies without a chance for a big return.

The shows she attended were some of the biggest and toughest in the country. Annie and Cash competed with the biggest players, placing alongside and beating them. By early summer she was sitting third in the national rankings. She qualified nationally to compete at the AQHA Youth World Championship Show held each year in Fort Worth, Texas, just 25 miles from my ranch.

The show held every August is the premier event for youth who show Quarter Horses. A championship league of kids and horses where the best riders in the country compete for a world title, the young riders traveled from all 50 states and a few countries to compete in the Texas heat. They came in droves with their support team: moms, dads, friends, trainers, brothers, sisters, dearly loved dogs and mascots of choice. Like the open and amateur World Championship Shows, the kids have to qualify in order to be eligible for competition.

Most of the youth who came to compete qualified through one of the 50 state affiliates, meeting the affiliate's requirements for eligibility to show. A handful, less than the top 10 percent, qualified nationally by earning enough points to be invited by the American Quarter Horse Association. Qualifying nationally, especially with such a limited show schedule, was quite an accomplishment for my star student, Annie.

More than 2500 exhibitors and horses came to Fort Worth, hopeful with expectations. Innocent young dreamers brought idyllic notions of how the week would progress and what the outcome could mean. They frolicked with friends, ran for National office, decorated stalls, entered speech contests, played horse bowl and tried like hell to win a World Champion title before Mom and Dad sold their horse. Over-achievers and under achievers alike roasted in the August heat as they prepared for their biggest competition.

Excited and nervous with energy to burn, much time invested and time running out, these ambitious talented young adults were under a tremendous amount of pressure. Many had limited time remaining in the youth division; some parents worried about the money pressuring their kids to work harder for a win that would add value to their horse's worth. Several trainers coached aggressively, as their *own* futures rode in a child's hands.

For Annie, the Youth World marked the end of her showing horses. Cash would be sold when Annie left for Sewanee University in Tennessee the coming September. Yet Annie showed no outward signs of stress. With the Will Rogers Coliseum in our backyard, Annie and Cash were familiar with the surroundings. They grew up showing in Fort Worth so the grounds themselves, held no mystique.

The team had shown against and beat many of the top ranked horses in the nation. Neither one of us had any doubt she would be in the finals. Many kids blessed with Annie's fortune grow cocky, but not Annie. Confident, she was graciously humble yet a determined competitor. We were excited going into the show. Annie and Cash had as much potential to take home the biggest prize, a youth World Championship, as any other kid. With anticipation on her heels, Annie entered the arena for her final performance on Cash.

True to their nature, they showed like the unflappable super stars they were. Cash trooped around the arena like he had when he won the Houston Livestock Show and Rodeo back in

February, beating them all. Unfortunately, in Fott Worth, the judges missed the modest pair and they came out of the preliminaries with a curt "thank you for showing."

Devastated for Annie, I did not know how to console her. Yet again, true to her form, she consoled me. We each wanted it so badly for the other, neither one of us were prepared for defeat. Truly disappointed for the other, neither of us could fathom Cash not making the cut. We loved this horse and assumed his talent was evident to all. Apparently it was not, because her number was not among those called back. We walked, boots dragging, heads down, back to the barn.

Feeling like nobodies in a world of somebodies, we drove in silence back to the ranch, our hearts heavy. Thrown for a loop, the loss shook her; the disappointment dampening her spirit. While she could have been angry at the judges, begrudged those who made the finals, resentful of the pompous and self-righteous, she was none of those things.

Instead, she was grateful for the time she'd had with horses and the joys they had brought to her life. She was happy to know in her heart that, on any given day, she could compete with the best of them and beat any one of them. Resolute in her purpose, Annie held her head high with intent. She proceeded on her path with the wisdom of a winner, vigilance of a fighter and the humility of the pious.

She was the same person whether she suffered a defeat or conquered the competition. Gracious, perceptive, intuitive and intelligent, she knew taking a loss did not make her a loser. She handled her loss with as much grace and composure as any competitor I have known, before or since — in spite of her youth.

True winners take a loss with grace

And never miss a beat.

A team of winners circa 1993: Stephanie, Jeanne (Perlich) White,
Christa Champlin, Nancy (Perlich) Kenway
Laurel (Raether) Champlin and Ezequiel Aguilar

A group of winners with trophies to prove it,
we were a unit; as sincere in our desire to win
as in our desire to be horsemen
and to win with integrity.

Photo Courtesy of Harold Campton

**Stephanie on Moose at the
All-American Quarter Horse Congress**

Breath is the gift of life;
And I clung to every breath with
full knowledge that my livelihood depended on it.

Chapter 22

Breath of Life

As much as I loved to jump, I never became very confident with it. Horses brought to me for training over fences usually behaved badly; they ran off with their owners, refused, didn't change leads, or simply failed to pass muster with accomplished hunter trainers. The good hunters in my barn were owned by talented riders whose need to show their horse exceeded my own.

In the 1980's Quarter Horse circuit, there were, at most, only two open classes for working hunters; junior horses, under five, and senior horses. Once the horse turned five years old, they graduated from the junior to the senior division, i.e. from a maximum of 3'3" to 3'9". A big jump – literally – for hunters; most hunter horses are not started over fences until they are four years old.

Moose arrived with an extremely confident, albeit eccentric, owner, a dubious work ethic and a skip change. The owner's peculiarity no doubt contributed to Moose's dismissal by trainers better than I. She did as she pleased, with, and especially without, the blessing of her trainers, making it difficult to do a good job for her. With only two slots available for open rides, trainers carefully filled their cards. Moose offered little hope of a big trophy in the open division. At six years of age, with habitual skip changes, a combination of a simple and flying lead change, Moose established a penchant hard to break.

When asked to change leads, Moose maintained a canter, performing a flying lead change with his front legs only. Behind, he broke to a trot, changing his hind lead with a technical break of gate. Breaking to the trot on course constitutes a major fault. Horses must first be on the correct lead around each corner and before a change in direction on course. A *flimple* lead change clearly indicated Moose's desire to transfer weight off his rear end, the power source, to his front end. Was he just lazy or did he have pain somewhere?

While not the most dangerous of faults in jumping, wrong leads are often the precursor to bad jumps. Jumping off of a wrong lead is cumbersome and approaching a jump from a cross canter can be downright dangerous. If all other contestants committed more serious faults, Moose could be considered for placing. A right riding course increased his odds of getting a piece of the prize as he always landed right. While Moose's owner, could often get a piece of the amateur classes, a skip change would prevent him from competing successfully at bigger shows, especially the Congress or the World Show.

Labeled the flying sofa for his smoothness, leaving the ground took effort for the 16'3 hand lazy chestnut gelding. A slug at best, he grunted over the jump his big head leading the way. Rather knobby and plain, sort of like a moose, he never the less, had talent and a heart of gold. Always cheerful, he rarely backed his ears — just a good guy. Like a kid, Moose was game to do anything as long as it did not involve work. Changing leads definitely constituted work. Moose struggled to change from his comfortable lead of preference to his left lead. All horses have a lead of choice. For Moose, the left lead, charged with tension and maybe a little painful, made his right lead his lead of choice.

I loved having Moose in my care. He provided an excellent opportunity for me to broaden my jumping skills with more trips around the pen. Moose's owner, always so sure of herself, had faith in my ability to get Moose shown and generously indulged my desire to show over fences. Entries for the All-American Quarter Horse Congress are due in August. Someone has to be listed as rider at the time of entry. Thinking we would find a suitable "catch" rider before show time, we entered Moose in the Senior Working Hunter with my name listed as the rider. Catch riders pick up horses to show at the horse show. Most often riding someone else's slack, or extra horses, they rarely have sat on the horse prior to the horse show. We thought we would find a more accomplished hunter rider to show Moose at the Congress prior to the class.

For Quarter Horse working hunters, the Congress was definitely the biggest event of the year. With more than 15,000 entries, the Congress is considered one of the largest events in the USA. The show brings in over $100 million to the central Ohio economy, attracting more than 500,000 people. More than 5,000 horses come to compete in the world's largest single breed horse show. Bragging rights are highly sought after and wins are recorded on a Quarter Horse's permanent show record. Truly a three-ring circus, the show is huge with multiple rings competing at any one time. In its early days there were only two rings to show in and classes often ran into the wee morning hours. Held in October, the unpredictable weather can be anywhere from summerlike to a bitter winter's cold.

It was after midnight and snowing the year I showed Moose in the Congress Senior Working Hunter. Never being one who liked the cold, I wondered what on earth I was doing there. I felt completely out of my league preparing for the class. Once in Ohio, we were unable to find a catch rider for Moose. The most sought-after hunter riders remained committed to other horses and were unable to ride Moose in my place.

Out of my element, I schooled under a huge overhang that ran the length of the trade show building next to the coliseum. Huge snowflakes were swirling around, blowing in between the overhang and the coliseum where the class ensued. Riders, yelling an occasional "heads up to the ......" were criss-crossing each other's path trying to get to one of the three measly jumps provided for 75 exhibitors to school over. The scene was chaotic. Hunters tried to get to the jump and land without running into or landing on top of horses practicing for other events. Exhibitors, riding in the middle of the night to avoid the crowds, waited for classes to finish, enabling them to school in the show pens. Their presence added to the mass confusion under the windy overhang.

Even for the most practiced hunter rider, the warm up pen can be a dangerous place. It was disastrous for me. Ground help hiked the jumps up over 4' in an effort to keep horses legs up over the jumps once in the show arena. Shivering in the cold, I had no ground person to help me, lower the jumps or settle my shaky nerves.

After a particularly BIG miss where I landed over the saddle on Moose's neck, I overheard someone ask a friend if they thought I was okay. At that point, I knew practice was doing more harm than good. About to lose it, I had to leave. The madness left me nervous, behind the motion and close to catastrophe. As Moose landed on the other side of an enormous jump, he barely missed landing on top of a little western horse, and I decided to quit.

Not forever — I just had to get out of the schooling area.

Deciding to stand in the alley way of the coliseum to get my act together, I wrapped a cooler around Moose's hip and my legs, warming myself while I watched the riders before me show. Slowly, with deliberate prolonged breaths, I put myself in their irons envisioning myself riding their ride. Going deeper in this corner, holding Moose straight before a predictable lead change, pressing up harder out of the diagonal corner, I imagined myself making all of the correct decisions. Breath in, breath out. Jumps were met accurately and lead changes asked for were answered with precision as I put myself in the rider's stirrups. One jump after another, one breath after another, I rode Moose in my mind creating the picture perfect ride in my head. With each breath I asked for the strength to stay on course thanking God for watching over me.

In due course, it was our turn to show. Throwing the cooler over a nearby rail, I walked in a small circle talking to myself, reminding myself of all the things I had to do. Inhaling deeply as I trotted through the entry gate atop Moose, I sucked in all the faith I could find, exhaled and got on pattern.

The first fence was a single vertical coming home, toward the gate. It was an easy fence set to allow the rider to build a good working hunter pace as the horse sped toward the out gate. It worked exactly as planned for Moose. Once established, maintaining the rhythm became the challenge. If Moose lost pace, he would get lazy and drop a lead. The course was, thankfully, right riding; his good lead — the one that Moose *always* landed on.

Continuing on the course, we jumped up the diagonal line heading to our first lead change. As expected, Moose landed right. With effort, I held his shoulder straight and completed the lead change without skipping a beat. Clean. Keeping the momentum up around the corner, we headed for the last line along the outside wall away from the gate. Jumping into the line accurately, Moose easily sailed down the line towards the tricky last lead change and last fence of the course.

Set at a precarious angle coming off of a sharp turn, the last fence was a single oxer. The challenge arose from the short distance between the end of the preceding line and the approach to the last fence. Requiring a lead change, it was imperative that Moose hold right until the lead was changed. I stayed down on my heels, hugged the wall and executed the lead change correctly. Unfortunately the time it took to complete the change made the ensuing turn too tight.

With his energy waning, Moose met the fence in slow step after backing off through the tight turn. My adrenalin tapped, relieved at meeting all the jumps squarely and hitting all the changes, I relaxed. Softening my leg, I did not press hard enough off the ground. Moose lazily hit a rail, bringing it down with a hind leg. Although disappointed, for the chance of placing was gone with the rail, I was thrilled with the ride.

Never did I miss a distance, jump ahead or get left at the base of a jump. Immersed in my vision, the course rode just as imagined. Almost — in my minds ride, I showed until the very end. Although the real ride lacked the grandeur it needed for a prize, I put together a decent trip after schooling shamefully.

Before undergoing anxiety ridden affairs, I remember that ride. Burning the image of the results I want in my mind, I inhale deeply. With force, I empty my lungs entirely and dig into the work at hand - and push to the end.

Breath gives life to everything
your hopes, your dreams, your fantasies and fears.
It is the Spirit within you:
yours to take in, yours to expel

An aerial photo of my Texas ranch, circa 1985

Home, there is no place quite like it. Whenever I drove into the driveway, a breath couldn't help but escape, grateful to be home, to my happy place: grateful to have an opportunity to fulfill my dreams and provide a living for myself and others.

Stephanie with Little Billy in the spring of 1970
The horse that started the lifetime affair.

Although far from beautiful, graceful or elegant,
Little Billy was, indeed, the best horse for the Lynn girls.
Murph's instincts were spot on — proving once and for all that
he was a true horseman. Billy may not have been the fanciest
pony at Murphy's Stable, but he was more than good enough
for this little Lynn girl.

Chapter 23

Good Enough

It was our second show season with Fred. The first year had been marginally successful; lots of wins but no World Championship. Fortunately, at Kerith's urging, we had a second year. The journey so far was full of fun, new experiences and lots of lessons. Fred's arrival in the show ring created a lot of talk, earning accolades from our peers. The judges liked him, he was performing well and we were taking home prizes.

Back in Tucson, where just one year prior Fred had been delivered to us, we were at the Blue Ribbon Circuit. Hosted by Blue Ribbon Tack, it was the second largest show in the nation. National leaders, those on a quest for a title, congregated trying to earn points as well as the accolades received from a win at this important show. Twelve hundred horses, along with their owners, trainers and riders, gathered from all four corners of the country to compete for one of the many fabulous trophy saddles, bronzes or prizes given to winners. Seven rings contained the herd, all of whom wanted a piece of the prize.

My show string was strong. The years had been good to me, providing a great group of owners, riders and horses. All were happy — they were all winning! But that year, the one who garnered the most attention was definitely Fred. He was big with an imposing stature; nearly black, his good looks were arresting. Fit as a fiddle, his hair coat shined and his white blaze contrasted sharply against his dark head. He remained vigilantly attentive. Always on the alert for opportunities to cause mischief, Fred had panache.

Kerith and Fred were competitive in several amateur events and won a few all-around awards on their journey to the AQHA World Championship Show. He was a beautiful mover with great rhythm — inciting a smile when you rode him. Kerith and I teased each other, not wanting to look cheesy by showing a big toothy grin. But you couldn't help but smile when you loped on Fred. The judges enjoyed watching Fred, too. He won amateur classes from Showmanship to Equitation and Trail with Kerith while I showed him competitively in the open classes. The class that was his, the one he drew the most attention from, was the Western Riding.

Like figure skating, Western Riding combines the elegance of ballet with the dexterity of athleticism performed with eloquence. The horse performs lead changes every few strides on a choreographed pattern. Shown in a western saddle, the horse is judged on quality of gaits, precision, response to the rider, manners and disposition. The horse is rewarded for smoothness, free flowing movement, simultaneous lead changes, even cadence at the lope and, of course, its looks.

The most graceful lead changes are nearly imperceptible to the casual observer and garner the highest scores from the judges. Blessed, Fred had that kind of lead change. Add his elegant look and he was a show horse and a serious contender in the Western Riding, perhaps even a horse ahead of his time.

Plus, he was just plain fun to sit on. Even when his capricious nature made him spook from a flower, jump a log, add an extra lead change or knock over a cone ending the class with a disqualification, it was hard to get mad at him. I joked that Fred either won or was disqualified. There were no in-betweens with Fred. Always, we knew he had a big win in him.

In Tucson, Fred performed like the star he could be. He earned a first and two seconds during the first few days of the show. Colleagues began saying we were the "ones to beat" come November. Compliments from competitors, friends and spectators amassed, weighing heavily on my conscience. I felt we were *far* from perfect. I knew the horse had what it took to win a World Championship, but I was not sure I was good enough.

The good wishes together with peers' confidence in my ability to win in Oklahoma City were appreciated. The reality was, their words terrified me. Always at my best as the underdog, from the start, this horse came with high expectations. And not just from his owner. Fred's talent, evidenced to all with a look, put pressure on me I had not dealt with before. Like putting the cart before the horse, I felt the certainty of my peers probabilities unjustified until I wore the buckle. The flattering words put me in a conundrum. While I would defiantly defend my ability, knowledge and methodology, deep down, I feared choking under the pressure of the expected win.

Fortunate to always have good friends, it is by design I have surrounded myself with great people. Their knowledge, friendship and counsel have made my life meaningful, clearing a path for my passage and allowing me to flourish. Turning to the salvation I have come to depend on – I sought trusted counsel. Just the previous day, Jason Martin helped me with Fred and our lope log. Now, I had to confess my fears to my long standing mentor, Sandra Vaughn. She asked where the holes in my performance were and we proceeded to the practice pen.

Pretty soon Sandy said "Good enough. Put him up for today." Balking, I had lots of "buts." But Fred didn't hold his shoulder up, but we slowed to the third change, but what about the log, but he twitched an ear, but, but, but. "Good enough for today," she snapped with a piercing glare.

The next day after arriving before the sun, breaking ice in water buckets and helping my students show all day, it was finally our turn to show. As our class approached the sun slowly descended over the huge Saguaro cactus returning the cool to the high desert air after a blazing hot sunny March day.

Dusk is never a good time to show a horse. Close to feeding time, the shadows seem to invoke fear in horses. Previously innocent cactus, garbage cans, fodder for food and fun in daylight and foliage, suitable for consumption earlier in the day, suddenly came to life after dark, striking terror in the horse's mind. They find the silliest things to spook at and Fred, white around one eye, was spooky by nature.

Our twilight ride started out as they often did. Indifferent, Fred lazily dragged a hind leg over the jog log but picked up the lope precisely at the marker. As we started down the line, Fred raised his tail, leaving big green apples in his wake as he inevitably did. Pressing on – I kept riding. The judges, after all, did not know that Fred's apparent inconvenient lapse in bowel control was actually a habitual premeditated act of insolence. Fred let me know, emphatically, that he was tired, ready for supper back at the barn and he had enough fun for one day.

Remembering the previous day's lesson, along with all the other words of wisdom received from peers, I pressed on. Our run finished with only the slightest of imperfections. As we exited the arena I immediately began criticizing my performance, vocalizing all of our shortcomings to my unsympathetic friend, Sandy. Sitting on her own horse, she had watched with a critical eye. We walked side by side back towards the barns. Tired of listening to me whine, her rebuke was simple yet pointed, "It's a horse show! Of course you weren't perfect."

How many times had I said these exact words to my clients?

The results were called and I won under both judges. With a fixed stare, my friend chided, "Well, you're right, you were not perfect. But on this day, you were good enough." Sandy slapped me on the back as we turned and went our separate ways to finish our nightly chores. She knew I would take her words home, ride hard, practice harder and find the significance of her message. Ambling back to my own stalls, I patted Fred on the neck and thought about what she said; feeling good enough. It was after all, only March.

That fall in Oklahoma City, Kerith and Fred knocked over the cone in the amateur western riding disqualifying them from competing for a World Champion title. As usual, Fred won or was disqualified. Now the pressure to win was on me, implied or otherwise. After qualifying through our preliminary work, I was third to show in the finals. Third was not a great draw, but there was no way to change it — just cowboy up and ride.

Western riding is a scored event with scores announced after each horse's run. Most AQHA classes are scored from 0 to infinity with 70 denoting average. In 1995, western riding did not have a definitive scoring system. Judges simply gave a score based on guidelines from the official AQHA rulebook. My goal for the finals was a combined score of 220, translating to a 73 average. At a time when very few 73s were given in any class, the goal was ambitious although far from record breaking.

Fred and I entered the gates with the announcer's introduction. Decked out in a bright red jacket with black velvet buttons, collars and cuffs, I felt good. Fred looked awesome. No efforts had been spared in his grooming, comfort or preparation. Upon entering the arena, Fred's ears pricked forward and he obediently picked up a brisk jog stepping over the log clean. We then picked up the lope heading for our first change. Attentive, cadence established, Fred loped around the cones stealing hearts with each strike of his leg. Effortlessly, he floated, loping back and forth across the arena reaching, his front leg hanging, as he pointed his toe with style and ease through each change.

Circling the cone, signifying the start of the line, I felt Fred's rhythm change and his tail rise. Deliberately, I pulled my chin up, took a deep breath and pushed my hand forward – showing Fred's elegance to the best of my ability. Three strides past the cone, change; three strides change, three strides change until there were no more cones. Fred knocked it out down the line.

At the end of the pattern, just before the stop, was the dreaded lope over log. As the log loomed closer, marking the last obstacle of challenge, tension mounted (in me, not Fred). We were so close to the end. The gap was closing and something was going to have to give. We were going to be either long or short. I remembered the advice of my friend, Jason, sat deep in the saddle and, once again, pressed forward. Fred reached for the log making up a gap I had left. It was a little long but without a tick; not a penalty but it could result in a reduction in the score.

Crestfallen, I came out of the arena angry at myself; the ride was *far* from perfect. I mused, remembering only the last, and worst, part of the pattern. When I heard the score, 216, I became even more despondent. Kerith took her horse and rode him around the warm up pen in front of the show arena while we waited for the class to conclude. After everyone showed, all the exhibitors would be asked to ride back into the arena for the awards presentation.

Earlier that year, I became a closet smoker. Embarrassed by my filthy habit, angry at my inability to control the habit, I hid in the tack stall and smoked cigarettes, wiping my eyes. I smoked and cried and listened to the scores, World Champion John – score of 211, World Champion Doug – score of 210 ½, World Champion Chris – score of 208, and so it went until only one horse remained to show.

The last draw, considered the best draw, went to my friend, Jackie. She was a multiple World Champion in this event as well as a guru whose sage advice helped me through some rough spots more than once. With my score still leading, the self-imposed pity party had grown pointless. Fred would *at least* be a Reserve World Champion, yet I nervously smoked one more cigarette waiting for Jackie's score to be called out.

"Ladies and gentlemen, that will do it for the Junior Western Riding. Judges score for the previous horse is a 212. We thank you all for showing and will now invite all of the contestants back into the arena for awards presentation."

All of the contestants sat on their horses, tails to the rail, as the awards were presented. As I sat on Fred and watched my peers, the great trainers like Sandy, Jason and Jackie, file out in front of me to accept their awards, I had but one thought: 216 may not have been what I wanted, but on that day, in that arena, it was *good enough!*

> *Accepting good enough does not reject perfection;*
> *rather it acknowledges another step in*
> *the never ending pursuit of excellence.*

The Snooty Fox (Fred)
1995 World Champion Junior Western Riding
From left, Tara (Lombardo)Anderson, assistant trainer, Charlotte Berrier
Tiedt, Patti (Pronold) Campbell,
Kerith Welch, owner with her parents Don and Mary

It was an outstanding way to end one owner's exceptional journey. The thrill of the win — like nothing else. But it, too, is fleeting. Without people to share in your victory, winning is unfulfilling.

The people who have allowed me to share in their journey to the winners' circle have made my life meaningful, given me purpose and brought me great joy.

About the Author

Stephanie accepting the trophy after winning
Senior Pleasure Driving at the
2009 AQHA World Championship Show

Stephanie Lynn was born and raised in Eau Claire, Wisconsin. She is a graduate of University of North Texas in Denton, Texas and has been a professional horseman since 1979. She currently shows, judges and coaches working primarily with Quarter Horses. She divides her time between Lake Weir, Florida and Fall Creek, Wisconsin with her husband.

QUICK ORDER FORM

Website: stephanieannlynn.com

Fax Form: 1-715-877-3250

Email Orders: stephanie@stephanieannlynn.com

Postal Orders: Mail this form along with check or money order:

Birddog Productions
PO Box 306
Fall Creek WI 54742

Name: _____

Address:_____

City: _____ State:_____Zip:_____

Telephone:_____

Email Address:_____

Credit Card: _____

Visa ☐   MC ☐ AMEX ☐   CVVC Code: _____

Signature:_____

Please make payable to Birddog Productions for $14.95 + 4.95 shipping and handling. Wisconsin Residents please add 5.5% sales tax.

Coming in the fall of 2012

First Love
An Excerpt

Charlotte loved Barney – and now it was time to say goodbye – not just to Barney, but to an era. Coming into her life during a lull, the seven years spent with Barney revived Charlotte and put purpose back in her days. Abandoned by those she trusted most, Barney allowed Charlotte to regain confidence so recently destroyed by the cruel words of so-called friends. At the same time, Barney's powerful personality pushed Charlotte to confront fears she was unaware she even had. Dressed up, Barney was as handsome as any. And when it came time to get tough, Barney could hold his own, get down and dirty with the best of them and, like a knight in shining armor, carry them both, wherever Charlotte wanted to go.

Although not her first love, Barney fulfilled more dreams than Charlotte ever envisioned. He far exceeded her wildest imaginings, surpassing all expectations; he brought to fruition a childhood dream, one whose origins are unknown. For Charlotte's first love was for the horse.

As a toddler, Charlotte loved to crawl around on all fours, pretending to be a horse or riding her mother's ironing board as if it were her own horse while watching her favorite TV program, My Friend Flicka. Plunking a few dimes in Trigger, the coin-operated horse outside the grocery store, Charlotte's mother kept Charlotte occupied riding the yellow galloping mechanical horse while she did her grocery shopping for the week. At the age of four, while her father was stationed at Barksdale Air Force Base in Louisiana, Charlotte begged her mother to stop for the pony rides that were alongside the road. The ponies were trained to go in a circle, following the rails of the portable gates pinned together forming a chute. One chute contained ponies who walked, one held ponies who trotted and one held ponies trained to run. Charlotte always wanted to ride the ponies that ran.

Born in Florida, the daughter of an air force officer, Charlotte moved often. Each time the Berrier family picked up stakes, Charlotte left friends and any hope of riding behind. The inevitable move left her alone in her dreams but deepened her desire to ride horses. During family vacations, Charlotte did her best to spend time with any horse she could get her hands on – even if it meant riding a mule.   Her grandfather in North Carolina plowed his small farm with mules and would let Charlotte ride them when they visited. He would put a burlap sack on Mike or Jerry's back, give Charlotte a switch made from a nearby Willow tree branch and send her on her way.

By the time she was thirteen, Charlotte had lived in Japan and numerous states. From Alabama to Ohio, Texas and Wyoming, the only constant in Charlotte s life was her love for horses. Charlotte's favorite assignment had been Utah. Living there for six years, it had been the longest assignment Charlotte had known. While stationed in Utah, Charlotte's parents bought a ranch in the neighboring state of Wyoming. Although the Berrier's did not own a horse, their neighbors did and Charlotte jumped at every opportunity to go to the ranch where she could ride the neighbor's horses after finishing chores at home. While stationed in Utah, Charlotte's father acquiesced and allowed Charlotte to have a horse. The base had a stable where the air force personnel kept their horses. Most of the horses never left the base; instead they were simply transferred from one owner to another when the airmen were transferred to a new assignment at another base.

Charlotte's horse, Sparky, a half Morgan and half Quarter Horse, was old, mean and barn sour. He hated leaving the barn and would rear up, standing on his hind legs, whenever Charlotte tried to take him on a trail ride. The rearing never slowed Charlotte down, she kept kicking her heels against his big barrel until Sparky finally gave in and moved away from the barn.

Charlotte joined the local 4-H club and decided to enter the little horse show the club held once a month during the summer. She won several ribbons at her only childhood horse show. Determined to win a blue ribbon, Charlotte nearly collapsed from a lack of oxygen as she jumped into a sack and furiously hopped across the finish line, pulling Sparky close behind, to win the sack race.

Unfortunately, just three months after Charlotte got Sparky, her father was sent to Vietnam. Charlotte, her little sister and mother were sent to live in Texas while her father was out of the country. Just when Charlotte's dream of owning a horse would finally come true, she woke up stationed yet again, at another air base, one without a stable. Dreams of owning a horse squashed, Charlotte moved her framed ribbons from home to home longing for the day when she would get to ride another horse. Charlotte's father eventually retired to their Wyoming ranch where he purchased a ranch horse for himself and a pony for Charlotte's little sister, who never shared the same love for horses. But for Charlotte, it was too late, she had already moved off to college and away from home.

Charlotte never gave up her childhood dream of owning a horse, and at age twenty two...

First Love
Available October 2012